Destined to Prosper:

Align your Biblical Financial Personality with Strategies to Build Wealth and Abundance

Destined to Prosper

Dr. Chonta T. A. Haynes

Copyright © 2020 by Dr. Chonta T. A. Haynes.

ISBN: 978-0-9991733-7-4   eBook

ISBN: 978-0-9991733-6-7   Paperback

All rights reserved. No portion of this eBook or Paperback may be reproduced, stored in a retrieval system, or transmitted in any form or by any means – electronic, mechanical, photocopy, recording, scanning, or other – except for brief quotations in critical reviews or articles, without the prior written permission of the copyright owner.

Unless otherwise indicated, all Scripture quotations are taken from the *Holman Christian Standard Bible*, Copyright © 1999,2000,2002,2003,2009 by Holman Bible Publishers. All rights reserved.

Scriptural references marked KJV are from *The Holy Bible, King James Version* ®KJV® Copyright © 2004, 1986, 1983 by Thomas Nelson, Inc. All rights reserved.

Scriptural references marked NIV are taken from the *Holy Bible*, New International Version ®NIV ® Copyright © 1973, 1978, 1984 by the International Bible Society. Used by permission of Zondervan Publishing House. All rights reserved.

Scriptural references marked AMP are from the Amplified Bible ®, Copyright © 1954,1958,1962,1964,1965,1987 by The Lockman Foundation. All rights reserved.
This book was printed in the United States of America.

To order additional copies in any format, contact:

Heart 2 Heart Truth Ministries, LLC

1-813-299-2742

H2HTruth.org

Other Books by Dr. Chonta T. A. Haynes:

Divinely Connected Series

Not Just Paper

Financial Wisdom For Financial Freedom

Family Worship: Reaching All Who Attend

Special discounts are available on quantity purchases by corporations, associations, educators, and others. For details, contact the publisher at the above listed address.

U.S. trade bookstores and wholesalers: Please contact Heart 2 Heart Truth Ministries Tel:(813)299-2742 Fax:(813)986-9660 or email drhaynes@h2htruth.org

Acknowledgment

God, in His infinite wisdom, has chosen earthly vessels to entrust with His treasures. He gives us the power and ability through creative means to impart and impact the lives of many. I thank God for the souls who will be touched and transformed by understanding how He made them. I thank God for using me in the capacity He has as He continues to develop me into a vessel fit for His use.

I am so grateful to those who continue to support the work I have been called to perform. Family and friends, students and leaders, sisters and brothers, without each of you this work would be incomplete. Thank You!

For the tribe that will search the Scriptures and these pages for divine wisdom, may you be so enlightened that you share with others. It's time that we change the economic footprint and walk in our rich inheritance.

Colossians 3:23

Thank You Supporters

MaryAnne Andrews

Erik Andrews

Erika N. Bethune

Jacquelyn Bogen

Denise Y. Bryant

Lloyd Butler

Dr. Sharon A. Cannon

Betty Davis

Vanessa M. Fisher

LaRae Floyd

Machelle Haynes

Kisha Heron

Malaika Lesesne

Mary Lesesne

Mirtha Petit

Jane Ricks

Terry Parker-Roe

Wanda Seigler

Cora Simon

Michelle Y. Stone

Stan and Andrea Thornton

Dr. Danielle Wainwright

Patricia A. Washington

LeNelda Woodard

Table of Contents

Introduction 1
Mindset 6
Avatars 21
    STEAM 21
    WATER 24
    ICE 25
    FIRE 27
Biblical Financial Personality Quiz: 39
STEAM: 43
    SCRIPTURE LESSON: 45
    OBSERVATION: 46
    BACKGROUND INFORMATION: 47
    INTERPRETATION: 49
    APPLICATION: 50
    MINDSET: 53
    GOAL SETTING: 58
    BUDGETING: 63
    DEBT REDUCTION: 65
    CONTEMPLATION: 67
    LIFE LESSONS: 68

- **WATER:** 71
  - **SCRIPTURE LESSON:** 74
  - **OBSERVATION:** 75
  - **BACKGROUND INFORMATION:** 76
  - **INTERPRETATION:** 80
  - **APPLICATION:** 82
  - **MINDSET:** 84
  - **GOAL SETTING:** 87
  - **BUDGETING:** 90
  - **SAVING:** 93
  - **DEBT REDUCTION:** 97
  - **CREDIT:** 98
  - **CONTEMPLATION:** 100
  - **LIFE LESSONS:** 103
- **ICE:** 105
  - **SCRIPTURE LESSON:** 106
  - **OBSERVATION:** 108
  - **INTERPRETATION:** 110
  - **APPLICATION:** 111
  - **MINDSET:** 112
  - **GOAL SETTING:** 113
  - **DEBT REDUCTION:** 119
  - **CONTEMPLATION:** 120

- LIFE LESSONS: 128
- **FIRE:** 130
  - SCRIPTURE LESSON: 133
  - OBSERVATION: 134
  - INTERPRETATION: 138
  - APPLICATION: 140
  - MINDSET: 141
  - GOAL SETTING: 143
  - BUDGETING: 146
  - SAVING: 147
  - DEBT REDUCTION: 149
  - CONTEMPLATION: 150
  - LIFE LESSONS: 153
- **CHRISTIAN ENTREPRENEURS:** 157
  - STEAM: 157
  - WATER: 159
  - ICE: 161
  - FIRE: 162
- **COUPLES:** 165
  - 2 STEAM 165
  - 2 WATER 166
  - 2 ICE 167
  - 2 FIRE 168

STEAM & WATER	169
STEAM & ICE	170
STEAM & FIRE	171
WATER & ICE	171
WATER & FIRE	172
ICE & FIRE	172
Financial Assessment:	174
APPENDIX:	175

Introduction

This isn't your typical money book. It's also not a simplistic plan of what to do with your finances. No, this is a journey to understanding how God created you and how you relate to money and people. It's a guide to living authentically and stressing less as it relates to finances.

Our relationship with money says a lot about us. There are many books on mindset and the importance of how you think. It's true that we should guard our hearts (Hebrew *leb*; one's inner self; inclination; disposition; determination; will; intention; attention) for out of it flows the issues of life (Proverbs 4:23). Guarding the heart determines what you say, what you see, and what you do. It is how you present yourself because of your thinking. You must satiate your heart with wisdom and what is good in God's eyes. We will cover that mindset from God's perspective. Our personality adds a bit of flavor to motivation and mindset.

According to Psychology Today, 'personality traits are characteristics that relate to the factory settings of our motivational system. They determine what we tend to be motivated to do in the absence of a strong influence of the situation' (10/7/2019). They even note factory settings or God given qualities. It's how you are originally wired.

There have been many studies on money personalities that look at categorizing us as spenders or savers. Much can be learned by this simplistic one side or the other side labeling, but it leaves one with questions as to what to do with the information. It's the classic 'then what' scenario.

Biblical financial personalities is a twist on the general personalities and it takes into account one's God given giftings. Are you generous, meticulous, detailed oriented, outgoing, free spirited or a visionary? I'm sure you'll agree that no one thinks like you. You are unique and special because God made you that way. Embrace it!

There are great qualities that God placed in you, many gems that sometimes are hidden. Scriptural references are associated and studied to give clues as to positive attributes and warnings.

We will merge Bible study with financial wisdom to give you an action plan for WHAT to do while bringing you closer to understanding HOW God created you. Can you use these giftings in other areas? Absolutely! You aren't limited to the area of money management, and you are encouraged to find your God given purpose. These personality types should be used simply as a tool to put feet to your faith so you can walk victoriously.

Throughout this study, you will be given a personality with an avatar, the persona that embodies a conglomerate of individuals (the names have been changed to protect the innocent). You may see traits of yourself in all four types so don't limit yourself. A full Bible study of the associated personality with the Scriptural references are included. Go ahead and get your Bible. Each study deals with mindset, goal setting, budgeting, saving and debt reduction, with specific areas of concentration for that particular personality. Life lessons rounds out each of the sections for empowerment.

We'll start with a quiz. This will allow you to assess yourself and identify traits you possess. Again, you may fit into many of the categories so don't limit yourself in the actions you take to improve. Make sure you know first your dominate category.

There are four different areas that you're going to progress through. First, OBSERVATION. Get out your magnifying glass and dawn your Sherlock Holmes cap. You are CSI, a Christian Scripture Investigator. There are many clues so look carefully. This is where you walk the dusty roads, sit among the Bible characters, feel the heat and take notes.

Step two, INTERPRETATION. Along the way, the background information will be given along with thoughts referencing other areas of God's wisdom. Knowing the WHY and the information brings it all into focus. So watch out for nuggets of interpretation and keys that you can use.

Step number three, APPLICATION. Specific areas within money management will be highlighted. Those budgeting aspects will be inserted for you to make the necessary applications. Faith without works is dead, so we are going to put feet to our faith. This is where the rubber meets the road as they say. You'll be challenged, encouraged and enlightened on areas to maximize your money management skills. Let's get moving.

And the fourth area, CONTEMPLATION. Answer all the questions to get to the heart of the matter, your heart. This time of reflection gives you the opportunity to communicate with God regarding changes you need to make. This is where the intimacy of the study takes place. After you've searched, allow God to search you.

Ready to take the mask off and find out WHO you are? This study promises to reveal WHY you do what you do and HOW you can adjust to get the financial abundance you WANT. Turn the page and let's begin.

Suggested for group study:

Week 1: Mindset

Week 2: Avatars & Quiz

Week 3: STEAM

Week 4: WATER

Week 5: ICE

Week 6: FIRE

Week 7: Christian Entrepreneurs

Week 8: Couples

- Teaching videos: Biblical Financial Personalities Masterclass: Principles + Practice For Freedom (sold separately)
- Leader Kit includes book and course

Initial Financial Assessment:

- ☐ Written Financial Goal – Y/N
- ☐ Written Family Goal – Y/N
- ☐ Balanced Budget – Y/N
- ☐ Cash $ _____
- ☐ Emergency Fund $ _____
- ☐ Savings $ _____
- ☐ Debt $ _____
- ☐ Credit Score _____
- ☐ Investments $ _____
- ☐ Net Worth $ _____

TO DO:
_____
_____
_____
_____
_____

Mindset

Your mindset is your belief system or your paradigm in which you make decisions. It's the internalized messages that drive your behavior. It's the way you approach earning, saving and giving.

Your money mindset is a set of beliefs you have that are revealed in how you interact with money and people. Simplistically speaking, you can have either a scarcity mindset or an abundance mindset. It is an abundant, expansive universe verses a fierce competition for scarce resources. God designed you to prosper and walk in a rich inheritance. Jesus died for you to enjoy your life to the full until it overflows (John 10:10, AMP). Abundant thoughts should be our norm; yet limiting beliefs invade. These are shaped from familial relationships and environmental structures. Can we correct thoughts that limit our potential? Yes! We are charged to renew our minds (Romans 12:2).

Our thoughts when lined with Biblical wisdom manifest the promises of God.

Past experiences and environmental influences affect your thoughts and form your beliefs. It was our upbringing and those we associate with that shape much of our beliefs which result in behavior. Behaviors become habits. We do because of what we believe and that goes back to what we think. Some of our thoughts need to be tweaked to create a secure financial future.

There's a difference between a worldly attitude toward money and Kingdom principles. It's important to understand what the world and its system is influencing our thoughts and shaping our financial decisions. If you want to grow to maximize your financial portfolio, you'll need to replace the thoughts of the world with those of the Kingdom.

Worldly

- W - Won't have it in the future (fear / hoarder)
- O - Owe me (entitlement)
- R - Remember my needs (selfish)
- L - Look at me (show off - keeping up with the Jones')
- D - Desperate (whatever it takes)
- L - Learned it before (know it all)
- Y - YOLO - You Only Live Once (wasteful)

Worldly Mindset: worried, lack, poverty, limitation, financial insecurity and uncertainty; broke mindset. 'There's never enough', 'Money doesn't grow on trees', 'I can't afford it'

The WORLDLY mindset includes the following:

> Scarcity mindset is one that operates as if there is a limitation of resources. Comments like 'money doesn't grow on trees' and 'we can't afford that' teach this poverty mindset. This shows up in the 'I won't have it available in the future' thoughts which operate from fear. One result of this fear is hoarding. Holding onto money with a tight fist because there is a limited supply is the behavior demonstrated by worldly thinking.
>
> The entitlement mentality is a function also of the world. It's the attitude that something is owed just because of birth. It's not based on what was earned or sacrifices made to receive. It's a 'give me, hand held out attitude. There's a touch of selfishness with an arrogant expectation.
>
> The selfish attitude is one that is prevalent from birth requiring others to focus on your needs. A child is unable to care for themselves. The constant need and high maintenance are understandable. As one comes of age; growth begins looking outward. This selfish mind demonstrates no concern for others but only an internal focus on self.

The show off behavior wants to appear as if all financial decisions have been perfect. It's one of looking the part and not necessarily living the part. The comparisons and the 'keeping up with the Jones" actions that has one making bad decisions from comparison. It's the one that says 'look at me, I want attention and acceptance'.

The desperate mindset is one that scrambles for everything. It's the 'whatever it takes I'm going to survive by any means necessary', because there is a limited supply. This behavior also views obtaining as a competition and taking it from you declares them the winner.

The know-it-all person believes they've learned it all before. This is an unteachable spirit that won't grow because they remain a legend in their own mind.

The 'I deserve it' thought process has moved many into great debt. The mindset of 'you only live once' leads to 'I might as well enjoy life'. It's a live for today and not focus on the future behavior that leads to wasteful living that results in a lack of abundance.

All these mindsets move individuals to scarcity because the focus is inward; hoarding, entitled, selfish, attention seeking, desperate, ignorant and wasteful.

Kingdom

- K - King is on the throne & the King will return (Stewardship)
- I - Invest wisely and not squanders
- N - Not covetous but content
- G - outlandishly Generous
- D - Debt Free or striving to be
- O - On Point - exactly right when it comes to living & giving
- M - My all belongs to God (time, talent & treasure)

Kingdom mindset: rich, secure, resourceful, generous and financially abundant, appreciative, confidence in your ability to make and receive money. Internal messages: 'There is always enough' 'It's only money: we can always make more' 'We have everything we need' 'I've got good money' 'There's always more where that came from'. It's a focus on what you can afford and 'enjoy the fruit of your labor'.

God calls us to have a Kingdom mindset which is one of prosperity and abundance. This mindset, backed by Scripture, encourages stewardship, investing, contentment, generosity, debt-free living, attention to detail and gratefulness.

Everything is other centered:

Christ will return and one should manage well what was entrusted to him (Matthew 25:14-30)

Investment brings increase and this is rewarded (Matthew 25:14-30)

Being content with what God has provided includes an attitude of gratitude (Philippians 4:10-13; 1 Timothy 6:6; Hebrews 13:5)

Generosity is a characteristic of our Heavenly Father and we should show the same spirit (1 Timothy 6:18; 2 Corinthians 9:6,11; Deuteronomy 15:10; Psalm 37:21; Psalm 112:5; Proverbs 11:25, 22:9)

Debt-free living, owing no one but to love him (Romans 13:8; Psalm 37:21)

On point with living and giving, doing it God's way (Proverbs 16:3, Psalm 37:5-6)

Recognition that everything belongs to God so seek Him and trust He will provide (Matthew 6:33; Psalm 24:1; Genesis 15:1)

The Kingdom mindset shows a dependence and a trust in the promise of God. If God is the provider (Jehovah Jireh) then there is an abundance since the earth is the Lord's and the fulness thereof (Psalm 24:1). When it comes to our attitude and ultimately our money mindset, as believers we should strive to eliminate worldly thoughts that cling to us and walk into a rich inheritance.

Kingdom vs. Worldly

- K - King is on the throne & the King will return (Stewardship)
- I - Invest wisely and not squanders
- N - Not covetous but content
- G - outlandishly Generous
- D - Debt Free or striving to be
- O - On Point - exactly right when it comes to living & giving
- M - My all belongs to God (time, talent & treasure)

- W - Won't have it in the future (fear / hoarder)
- O - Owe me (entitlement)
- R - Remember my needs (selfish)
- L - Look at me (show off - keeping up with the Jones')
- D - Desperate (whatever it takes)
- L - Learned it before (know it all)
- Y - YOLO - You Only Live Once (wasteful)

Mindset Questions…

What do you believe about money?
_____
_____
_____
_____

What thoughts are you saying to yourself about money?
_____
_____
_____
_____

What did your parents say to you about money?
_____
_____
_____
_____

What phrases to you hear regarding money as you grew up?

_____
_____
_____
_____
_____

Were you taught money management at home? __

Did you grow up with a scarcity mindset? _____

Do you think money is abundant or limited?

_____

How do your friends act when it comes to money?

_____
_____
_____
_____

When you go out with friends, do you pay for everyone or do you wait for someone to sponsor you? _____

What things are your friends saying in regards to money?

_____

_____

_____

_____

_____

Does your community have an abundance mindset?

_____

What is your community saying about money?

_____

_____

_____

_____

_____

Did you take a financial education course? _____

Are you afraid your finances will be short each month? _____

Are you afraid you won't have enough in retirement?

_____

Do you think your resources are limited? _____

Do you say things like 'money doesn't grow on trees' and 'I can't afford that' frequently? _____

Are you always counting pennies? _____

Do you only buy things on sale or clearance? _____

Are you worried/stressed about your finances? ____

Do you believe others owe you something? _____

Do you believe the family/government should support you? _____

Do you think your job owes you vacation pay, sick time, pension, retirement plan, school tuition, etc.? _____

Do you ask others to contribute to your financial well-being? _____

Do you believe family should always pitch in to help you with your financial burdens? _____

Do you believe company owners and managers make too much and don't pay you as an employee enough? _____

Are you satisfied with your pay? _____

Are you focused on yourself or do you consistently reach out to others? _____

Do you buy things to 'look the part'? _____

Do you post on social media the new possessions you acquire? _____

Do you buy things to keep up with others? _____

Do you buy things for acceptance? _____

Do you give to others for acceptance? _____

Do you find yourself competing with others and spending money to 'one up' them? _____

Do you find yourself making questionable financial decisions to make ends meet? _____

Do you think you know everything about how the money system works? _____

Are you teachable? _____

Are you open to learn more about financial education? _____

Are you wasteful with money? _____

Do you only focus on present finances? _____

Do you see money as a resource and abundant? _____

Do you believe you have the power to obtain wealth? _____

Are you content with what you have? (not complacent but satisfied) _____

Do you find yourself being grateful or complaining about your financial situation? _____

Do you believe that God has a rich inheritance for you? _____

Do you think you will always be in debt? _____

Do you believe God will supply all your needs? (not wants or desires but needs) _____

Do you view money as a tool? _____

Do you constantly think about getting more money? _____

Do you frequently ask family and friends to loan you money? _____

Do you freely loan/give others money? _____

Are you a charitable giver? _____

Do you frequently contribute to organizations and causes that benefit others? _____

Thoughts:

Scriptures for Meditation:

Kingdom Scriptures

- **K** - 1 Kings 17 - Miracle provision
- **I** - Isaiah 55:10 - Seed & provision
- **N** - Numbers 20:7-12 - From unexpected places
- **G** - Genesis 15:1 - Shield & exceeding great reward
- **D** - Deuteronomy 8:18 - Power to get wealth
- **O** - Obadiah 17-21 - The Lord is just & you shall posses
- **M** - Matthew 7:24-25 - God is my Rock

See the Appendix for additional Scriptures and add them in your prayers.

For 7 day financial prayer challenge sign up here: https://bit.ly/H2Hprayer

Additional Scriptures:

_____
_____
_____
_____
_____

Avatars

An avatar is an icon or figure representing a particular person. The names were selected to personify the character traits and thought processes that accompany the Biblical financial personalities. The acronyms are reasonable facsimiles for people you know. Don't forget to identify yourself.

The four categories include STEAM, WATER, ICE and FIRE. Distinctive yet similarities account for strong tendencies in more than one category. Use this to your advantage to transform your financial situation.

STEAM stands for Spend Thinking Emotionally About Memories.

This personality likes to be generous primarily giving to others with the expectation of relationship development. This leads to living for today, living outside ones means, people pleasing and enabling. It's a juggling act and a sticky financial scenario.

Meet **Sharon**; she just wants to have friends. She believes the best way to gain friends is to give. The problem is that she gives to everyone; every birthday, every company function, even just because. Every time you turn around Sharon has her wallet or credit card ready, thinking that as a people pleaser, everyone will eventually like her.

The problem is her budget can't support her overspending. Her 'living only in the now' mindset has a focus on what's easiest and most appealing now. Building relationships is a good thing but it's hard to make your money stretch once it's gone.

Sharon's people pleasing tendency also causes financial struggles. She thought that *"a man that hath friends must shew himself friendly"* (Proverbs 18:24, KJV), meant giving was the answer to gaining friends. She didn't realize that a deeper study (Hebrew language) warns that too many associations will bring one to ruin [*"A man of many companions may come to ruin" (NIV); "A man with many friends may be harmed" (HCSB)*]. The word friend was loosely translated in the King James Version (similar to today). In short, Sharon has a sweet personality and is a giver. What she needs to do is set a budget for her monthly giving and stick to it.

Now **Stephanie** has a different twist on being STEAM. See, Stephanie, like Sharon, wants everyone to be happy. She's a little more sensitive than Sharon, feeling the pain of others. She receives constant requests for assistance because their bills are late or they just need a little help. Well, Stephanie has a big heart; and she can't bear the fact that they are in trouble. She too pulls out her wallet to support others. She forgot that Galatians 6:2, *"Carry each other's burdens, and in this way fulfill the law of Christ' is followed by verse 5 'for each one should carry his own load (NIV)"*.

Bottom line, she thinks this spending will improve her relationships and she will have friends for life. Not only is she up at night, because she's barely managing her own bills. But she takes on their emotional baggage. If she, by some remote chance told them 'NO', call it an all-nighter. Stephanie has allowed their 'living outside their means' mindset to create emotional financial bondage for her.

Then there is **Sandra**, also a STEAMer. She's the defender of the people, especially family. She's the one called when their bills are due complaining it's too high and they've been wronged. Sandra wants great relationships and spends her time and money to make it happen; her money management skills need improvement. She helps everyone then has to juggle to pay her own bills.

Sandra allowed other people's priorities to overshadow her own. Her constant concern for others keeps her on edge. She also needs to let every person carry their own load.

Then there's **Stefan**, Mr. Victorious. You know him; he looks good and appears to be 'the man'. Well, that's what he wants you to think. He takes care of his wife and kids and also his siblings and parents. Stefan wants the image of being the 'go to' person. He wants to save the day.

The problem: he's playing three card Monte, juggling to keep his nice guy image. He wants to satisfy everyone and their needs while forgetting himself. He vacillates into the 'I deserve this' mindset at the most inopportune time; when his bank account is at its lowest. To keep his wife from finding out, he keeps separate bank accounts. The game continues, but the financial stress mounts.

Finally, there's **Steve**. He is the creative of the group, always giving and rarely on the receiving end. Unfortunately, Steve's chosen career doesn't allow for massive income; well, not yet. On his way to stardom, Steve figures he should plant seeds along the way. One day, he tells himself, it will pay off, so getting a second or third job is only temporary. After all, the Bible says you reap what you sow. (2 Corinthians 9:6)

Steve is overworked to say the least, not for his bills, but to support his so-called friends. It's a juggling act and the balls are beginning to drop.

The **WATER** personality which stands for Why Attend To Every Report.

This personality detests details and would rather 'wing it'. As you can imagine, the finances are in disarray. Shackles of debt from living above ones means isn't enjoying life.

Wanda, the wanderer is first. She's a good-hearted person, ready for adventure. If you're looking for companionship, she's your girl. She believes life should be enjoyed but just doesn't want to get caught up in the details. She tells herself it's too tedious and pointless. If she doesn't pay attention, maybe, just maybe it will go away. She completely overlooked the Scriptural admonition in Proverbs 6:6-11, *"Go to the ant, you slacker! Observe its ways and become wise. Without leader, administrator, or ruler, it prepares its provisions in* summer; it gathers its food during harvest. How long will you stay in bed, you slacker? When will you get up from your sleep? A little sleep, a little slumber, a little folding of the arms to rest, and your poverty will come like a robber, your need, like a bandit (HCSB)."

A budget and balancing her bank account are last on her TO-DO list so it never gets done. She figures she will always be in debt. Her theme song, 'Don't worry be happy'.

Let's look at **Wayne**. He wants life to be fun and exciting and has convinced everyone he is doing very well financially. He enjoys trying new things but he's not prepared for his future retirement. He has kept up the image of abundance for so long, he even believes it himself.

The problem: the crisis of unemployment became a reality. He was just one paycheck away from bankruptcy. Like so many, he just figured he would work all his life and the job would continue supporting his lifestyle. Unemployment and unexpected medical bills swallowed his little savings.

The House of Cards is crumbling, because his foundation was shaky; talk about not counting the cost (Luke 14:28). He doesn't even know quite where to begin and is overwhelmed.

Moving to the spending side of the avatars: **ICE** meaning I Can't Entertain.

Enter **Iris**. Iris is considered the ice queen. If you ask her for a loan, you're sure to get a NO! It's not that she doesn't have it, it's simply earmarked for something else. Iris lives tight to her budget, and very rarely veers off her goal. She's planned for the future but doesn't show any fun in the present. Life for her consists of spreadsheets and calculators. She can tell you exactly what she spent and where she spent it; yet she isn't enjoying life. When unexpected expenses arise; Iris is recalculating because late fees, she can't afford.

Don't ask for help, and you won't get your feelings hurt. She knows adults make a way to satisfy their wants and will gladly use your money to do it. A poverty mindset and living in lack may be a consequence of her upbringing she needs to release. Yes, she believes God shall supply all of her needs (Philippians 4:19); but she aims to help Him. No frivolous spending here, she's bordering on extreme frugality.

Now let's consider **Isaac**. Isaac is the man with a plan. He has his wife and kids on a strict budget. If you want to deviate from Sir Isaac's plan, you'll need graphs, pie charts and invoices. Isaac believes in 'waste not want not' and works hard. He's not about extras, but he wants to be known as the provider. As long as it's a basic need, Isaac has it covered. He has goals and is future focused, the present perks take a back seat to family provision. Don't ask this man to spot you $50 or he'll side eye you like you stole something. Let the kids ask, and it's daddy to the rescue. He'll just pull out the calculator again and rob Peter to pay Paul.

He's saved a little for retirement and the emergency fund; but for him, every penny counts. His motto stands behind Luke 14:28, *"For which of you if you, wanting to build a tower, doesn't first sit down and calculate the cost to see if he has enough to complete it?"*

Finally, the **FIRE** personality where the acronym represents Financially Independent Retiring Early.

The future focused abundant mindset navigates finances with finesse. This desired category is grateful for blessings and is set for success.

Felicia is on fire when it comes to her finances. She knew to save from an early age and she's on target to have her retirement fully funded in her 50's. Each quarter she reassesses her portfolio and makes sure she includes a treat for herself; spa day, trip or a massage. She is enjoying life. There is of course her emergency fund, and then the nine months of gross income just in case her boss gets stupid or her business has to pivot. She's a woman with a plan, and she's working it. Ask her for a loan, and she'll help you. She will require that you understand money management so you won't be back. She will teach you how to fish and not just give you the sandwich.

Her concern now is maximizing her investments. Felicia has an investment portfolio that may not be diversified. Her concern is retirement and how to make the money last as long as possible and who to entrust with her legacy (Proverbs 13:22). She's simply happy.

And finally, there is **Frank**. Frank is a free man. He can do what he wants when he wants. He's planned ahead and planned well. His financial advisor assures him of his secure financial future. Frank's concern is that he doesn't know how he did so well, and he wants to be able to teach his kids to do it better. He requires analysis for all projects so they see him as a taskmaster that lives in the future. He takes them on educational trips and doesn't appear to have a fun side. Frank splurges every now and then on basketball season tickets and electronic toys.

The problem his wife has is that the splurging seems only for him. His motto is that 'he worked hard and he deserves it'. If he could only loosen the reins just a little.

Now that we have covered all the avatars, I'm sure you found character traits that are similar to your thought process. Remember these are generalities and are adaptable. Make sure you identify your dominate personality trait but review all the suggestions. God made you unique. There is nothing wrong with your generous spirit nor your attention to detail. He knew you were a free spirit and creative as well as meticulous. All of these will come in handy. What is needed is an understanding of how these traits may cause concerns financially so that we can grab hold of key nuggets to maximize the positives and eliminate the negatives.

Avatar Questions ...

How are you like Sharon?

_____
_____
_____
_____
_____

Do you 'buy' friends? _____

Do you exceed your budget buying gifts for everyone? _____

Are your credit cards maxed out with gift purchases? _____

Are you a people pleaser? _____

Do you think money should be used to build relationships? _____

How are you like Stephanie?

_____
_____
_____
_____
_____

Do others tug at your heart strings and your wallet?
_____

Are you the one everyone comes to for financial help? _____

Are you paying bills for others? _____ Consistently?
_____

Are you up at night trying to solve everyone else's financial problems? _____

Are you juggling your finances to assist others? ___

How are you like Sandra?
_____
_____
_____
_____
_____

Are you the family rescuer? _____

Do you juggle your bills to meet the needs of family?
_____

Do you put your family's needs before your own?
_____

How are you like Stefan?

_____

_____

_____

_____

_____

Are you 'faking it until you make it'? _____

Are you overly concerned about your image? ____

Are you the financial 'go to' person? _____

Are you juggling finances to keep an image? _____

Do you buy gifts for yourself because you think you deserve it? _____

Do you hide money from your spouse? _____

How are you like Steve?

_____

_____

_____

_____

_____

Are you working multiple jobs to support others? __

Did you co-sign for someone and now are having to meet that financial obligation? _____

How are you like Wanda?

_____

_____

_____

_____

_____

Are you ready for adventure regardless of your financial situation? _____

Are late fees charged on your accounts? _____

Have you had your utilities cut off or car repossessed? _____

Have you defaulted on a loan? _____

Do creditors call you? _____

Do you have a legal judgement you must pay? ___

Do you complain about paying bills? _____

Do you rarely balance your bank account? _____

Do you avoid creating a budget? _____

Have you paid overdraft or insufficient funds fees?
_____

Do you believe you will always be in debt? _____

How are you like Wayne?

_____

_____

_____

_____

_____

Do you enjoy trying new things (restaurants, adventures, etc.)? _____

Are you inadequately prepared for retirement? ____

Do you focus on enjoying life today? _____

Do you give the impression that you have it together financially but you know it's not true? _____

Are you living paycheck to paycheck? _____

If you lost your job today, would you have enough to pay your bills next month? _____

How are you like Iris?

_____

_____

_____

_____

_____

Do you hold tight to money and refuse to loan or give to others who ask? _____

Do you have a tight budget? _____

Are you delaying fun today because you are saving for the future? _____

Do you have a balanced budget? _____

Do you plan financially for every event? _____

Are you detailed oriented when it comes to your finances? _____

Do you know your exact balances? _____

Do you struggle with trusting God for your financial future? _____

Are you frugal? _____

How are you like Isaac?

_____

_____

_____

_____

_____

Do you have a strict budget? _____

Do others need research and plans for you to deviate from your budget? _____

Do you have financial goals? _____

Are you the provider for your family and that makes you feel good? _____

Are you more future focused with your finances? ___

Do you juggle the bills to meet family expectations?

_____

How are you like Felecia?

_____

_____

_____

_____

_____

Do you have an abundance mindset? _____

Do you save regularly? _____

Have you accumulated money in several accounts? _____

Is your retirement fully funded or close to your target? _____

Do you regularly assess your financial portfolio? __

Do you treat yourself periodically? _____

Do you have an emergency fund? _____

Do you have at least 6 months gross income in liquid assets? _____

Do you teach money management skills to those who borrow from you? _____

Are you concerned about maximizing your investments? _____

Do you have an estate plan? _____

How are you like Frank?

_____
_____
_____
_____
_____

Do you have a fiduciary (financial advisor or registered investment advisor)? _____

Do you educate your children about finances or have that desire? _____

Do you splurge on events for yourself? _____

Do you think in terms of me or we? _____

What did you learn about yourself?

_____
_____
_____
_____
_____

What do you want to change?

_____
_____
_____
_____
_____

Biblical Financial Personality Quiz:

Which best describes you?

STEAM: Spend Thinking Emotionally About Memories

WATER: Why Attend To Every Report

ICE: I Can't Entertain

Or **FIRE:** Financially Independent Retiring Early.

Below are 4 sets of scenarios (categories) and 4 questions in each. Answer yes or no to each question. Once complete, total the number of positive responses.

Are you the type of person where lending and giving is your middle and last name?

Does it make you feel good all over to buy gifts?

Do you expect greater relationships because of your giving spirit?

Are your budgets okay but you're overspending on a regular basis when it comes to gift giving?

If this describes you, then you're my STEAM person. You Spend Thinking Emotionally About Memories.

You don't have a budget, and you prefer the freedom of not being so restricted.

You rarely plan for spending, but you just want to have fun.

You borrow when you really want an item or an experience, but you don't have a way or plan to pay it back.

And you seldom know how much money you currently have in the bank.

This would describe the WATER personality: Why Attend To Every Report

---

Do you have a spending plan that you consult, and you seldom deviate from it at all? You're very strict about it.

Do others come to you for loans, but you don't give in?

Do you have some savings, but you always feel overwhelmed that it's just not enough?

Do you desire to have more income to meet your current needs?

If these questions describe you, you're in the ICE category: I Can't Entertain.

Do you have a spending plan that you consult before making any gift or purchase?

Are you the one that others come to for a loan?

Do you have a secure savings and retirement that is almost fully funded, if not funded completely?

Do you understand money, investing, saving and the system and you're working within the system?

If that's you then you are what I describe as FIRE: Financially Independent Retiring Early.

Select the personality that closely matches a description of you. Each section has 4 questions so pick the one that you answered yes to most.

There's no wrong or right answer, whichever one described you, describes your personality and your spending. Based on your financial personality, there are some key things that you can do in order to maximize your money management so that you will be able to walk out the abundant life that God has planned for you.

For a more detailed questionnaire go to the online version: https://bit.ly/H2Hquiz

Quiz thoughts:

STEAM: Spend Thinking Emotionally About Memories

Avatars: Sharon, whose name means plain. Stephanie, the sensitive soul. Sandra, the defender of all. Stefan who is victorious. Steve, who is creative.

Personality: GIVER.

A friend of mine and I nicknamed March 'March Madness', because something would always occur in that month. It has nothing to do with the basketball season, though I like basketball and the March Madness competition. In March, it just seems that people come out of the woodwork asking for a loan, asking for money, asking you to pay their bills. Typically, it's because they figure in April when tax time comes around they will be able to pay you back. Now, out of the blue, they'll come up with the most extraordinary stories of why they need your money to help them. So STEAM personalities, be aware that in March, is a time of caution.

Another incident that might show the hand of a STEAMer could occur at church. When it's time for giving a special offering, someone may challenge others to meet or beat their giving. That's another ploy to get a STEAMer up. The STEAMer, valuing relationship and people pleasing may be urged to comply. It could be a needy family, that comes by just in time for Christmas or Thanksgiving. They truly could have been needy all along but many con artists do come out of the woodwork. So, beware.

Anytime there is a crisis, there's an opportunity for exploitation or opportunity to pull on your heartstrings and then you start opening up your wallet. In some instances, the requests are absolutely fact and they amount to great impact. But in some cases, with a deeper look, you'll find that the organizers actually the ones getting all the money. What you thought you were giving to impact a country, or a specific life, the amount of money actually contributed really doesn't amount to very much. Any special request is an opportunity for you as a STEAMer to think emotionally and spend emotionally rather than logically.

ANIMAL: Puppy

Let's look at the animal associated with the STEAM personality; the well-known puppy or the dog. They look cute with their sad eyes. They just want to be cuddled. They want love, they want affection, they want attention. You open the door and they're there right in front of you. This represents you as the giver. Many times, as a people pleaser, you just want others to see you, be affectionate towards you and to love you.

We all want love, right? It's one of our basic needs. Here are some warnings: The dog loves to be petted. They crave attention, but often they can end up being a people pleaser.

On a positive note: You love to give. You love the affection. You are truly generous. That's a good thing. But be warned, you need to be obedient to the Holy Spirit and not to your human spirit, or the emotional pulls of others.

There's another warning: Don't feel the shame. Don't do and don't feel like you're obligated to participate in everything or to give on a regular basis. Learn as a trained puppy would to have your ears attuned to listen. Hear what God wants you to do, and what He has purposed for you in life.

SCRIPTURE LESSON:

The Good Samaritan: Luke 10: 25 -37:

"Just then an expert in the law stood up to test Him, saying, 'Teacher, what must I do to inherit eternal life?' 'What is written in the law?' He asked him. 'How do you read it?' He answered: Love the Lord your God with all your heart, with all your soul, with all your strength, and with all your mind; and your neighbor as yourself. 'You've answered correctly,' He told him. 'Do this and you will live.' But wanting to justify himself, he asked Jesus, 'And who is my neighbor?' Jesus took up the question and said: 'A man was going down from Jerusalem to Jericho and fell into the hands of robbers. They stripped him, beat him up, and fled, leaving him half dead. A priest happened to be going down that road. When he saw him, he passed by on the other side. In the same way, a Levite, when he arrived at the place and saw him, passed by on the other side. But a Samaritan on his journey came up to him, and when he saw the man, he had compassion. He

went over to him and bandaged his wounds, pouring on olive oil and wine. Then he put him on his own animal, brought him to an inn, and took care of him. The next day he took out two denarii, gave them to the innkeeper, and said, 'Take care of him. When I come back I'll reimburse you for whatever extra you spend.' 'Which of these three do you think proved to be a neighbor to the man who fell into the hands of the robbers?' 'The one who showed mercy to him,' he said. Then Jesus told him, 'Go and do the same.'"

OBSERVATION:

When read in context, you know how Jesus answered the question, 'how do you inherit eternal life?'. The Good Samaritan story answers many key points. Notice that Jesus said we are supposed to love one another. He also distinguished that we're supposed to love our neighbor, but the question came up as to who is our neighbor? That question was posed because the young man did not want to take care of just anybody. Here are questions we need to ponder:

1. In verse 25, What must I do to inherit eternal life?
2. Verse 26, What is written in the law? And how do you read it?
3. Verse 29, Who is my neighbor?

BACKGROUND INFORMATION:
1. From Jerusalem to Jericho is about 16 miles so it's not a short distance when you're traveling on foot.
2. Robbers, by definition, are ones depriving another of their property openly and by violence; to plunder.
3. The young man was stripped, meaning he was unclothed. He was wounded and he was attacked. He was also left for dead. In other words, the robber departed and went away, leaving him there to the elements, and to whomever else came by.

Notice that some of the religiosity of the day, those who were supposed to be leaders passed by on the other side. They avoided helping the man that was in need, but yet the Good Samaritan stopped. Luke, as the only Gentile author of The New Testament, is writing to the Greeks to let them know that they are a part of the family of God. The Samaritans were considered the outcasts. They were considered half-breeds not really understanding and knowing the principles of God. The Good Samaritan demonstrated compassion (to feel deeply or viscerally to yearn for). There was pity and inner feelings regarding the young man. We also notice that he bandaged him (bound up his wounds). He wrapped his wounds equivalent to his hurts, synonymous with a blow or strike. (Note: these wounds can be physical or emotional) In today's terms, we might call it bullying. This young man, the Samaritan also poured olive oil and wine into his wounds. Those were for medicinal purposes. He smeared it on as a medical treatment, usually preceded by prayer and offering. Imagine him laying hands on this young man. He then put him on his own animal (used for riding or carrying his burden).

He brought him to the inn, a place where he lead or carried him where he could take care of him. He did just that, he took care. To take care is to concern oneself with the care of the incapacitated. The next day, he gave the innkeeper two denarii (that's two days pay of 12 hours each). Then the Good Samaritan left. He said, when I come back, I will reimburse you. In other words, I will repay, I will fulfill the obligation in which I had. I'm going to restore you, I will return your debt, and I will keep or perform my oath. There's a question in verse 36 posed to the listeners, 'which of the three do you think proved to be a neighbor?' Finally, Jesus commands us in verse 37b to go and do the same.

Additional Observation:

_____
_____
_____
_____
_____
_____

INTERPRETATION:

By definition, compassion is synonymous with pity; a feeling of distress from the ills of others, to suffer with another, to have mercy. Compassion is different in that it is moved to action. You don't just sympathize with their pain, you do something about it; to alleviate the consequences of sin or suffering in the lives of others, to bear, to moderate one's anger, to treat with mildness, moderation, gentleness, or to suffer with.

Those with a STEAM personality embody the word compassion. Some tips from Scripture include:

1) Care about others and do something about their circumstance. This means, we don't look away from, but we look into. As Jesus demonstrated being touched by the feelings of our infirmities, we should be touched by the feelings of others. See their need, their hurt, whether emotional or physical, we're asked to be Christlike and moved with compassion. We are to be other centered, to feel deeply about their concerns but not to the extent of people pleasing. One key fact, the Good Samaritan did show concern, and he was in a position to help.
2) The Good Samaritan also conducted his business. He participated in providing assistance but he did not neglect his business. Jesus said that we should emulate this.
3) Balance the emotion with logic.

Additional Thoughts:

_____
_____
_____
_____
_____
_____
_____
_____

APPLICATION:

Accentuate compassion, which is the care for others. We should always help, but do within reason. However, we should also complete our assignment.

Focus on completing your assignment, but do ministry as well. So, focus on our purpose, but be willing to be interrupted. You never know when there's a divine appointment. You should always be in a position to render assistance. So adequately prepare.

As it relates to finances, have your money management skills on point. One characteristic of a believer is that of a giver. We need to sow in good ground. We all have a little bit of this compassion, but you need to check your motives.

The extreme doing for others to the detriment of our purpose needs to be eliminated. People pleasing as a reason for giving, needs to stop. Being caught up in someone else's debt should definitely cease. The Bible records for us in Proverbs 11:15, that we should not be co-signing (to jointly sign a promissory note).

If you found yourself with these issues concerning money management skills, Financialopoly: Financial Wisdom For Financial Freedom online course will educate and empower you.

We also need to eliminate being taken advantage of or being used. No more Christian nice girl or Christian nice guy. Christian does not mean that you're a doormat.

In John 13, Jesus washing the disciples' feet, if you recall, he washes all the disciple's feet. Peter when approached by Jesus said, you're not going to wash my feet. Jesus responded, 'If I don't wash your feet, you have no part in me', that's around verse 8. Peter wanting to be connected responded, well then wash my whole body. Jesus gave clarity that if you've already taken a bath, basically, you don't need to bathe again, I just need to wash your feet. We have to remember that they were walking around in sandals at that time. It was dusty, it was dirty. It was normally the responsibility of the house manager, the person who owned the facility to have a servant come and wash the feet of their guests.

Jesus donned himself with a servant's towel and began washing the disciples' feet. And that's when this conversation ensued.

Additional Thoughts:

_____
_____
_____
_____
_____
_____
_____
_____

MINDSET:

Here are some questions that need to be pondered:

1) Why are you doing what you are doing?

   _____
   _____
   _____
   _____
   _____

2) Why are you giving?

   _____
   _____
   _____
   _____
   _____

3) What is your motive?

   _____
   _____
   _____
   _____
   _____

4) Are you being manipulated?

_____
_____
_____
_____
_____

5) Does this request occur regularly?

_____
_____
_____
_____
_____

6) Does this particular incident with this person happen on a regular basis?

_____
_____
_____
_____
_____

7) Is the request within your budget?

_____
_____
_____
_____
_____

8) What other resources are available to the requestor?

_____
_____
_____
_____
_____

9) Are they doing all that they can to fulfill their need?

_____
_____
_____
_____
_____

10) Is there some other resource they have at their disposal?

_____
_____
_____
_____
_____

Additional Thoughts:

_____
_____
_____
_____
_____
_____
_____

Don't do for others what they can do for themselves. If they have no skin in the game, they generally won't value what is given. Don't give in order to win friends, to find out information, to get on board, to gain prestige or to elevate yourself. Check your motives.

The other side of the equation and additional questions:

1) What are others doing for you?

_____

_____

_____

_____

_____

2) Are you allowing others to reciprocate?

_____

_____

_____

_____

_____

Be mindful that in John 13, as Jesus washed the disciples' feet, Peter stood up to say, there's a problem. Peter wasn't expecting a relationship that worked both ways. If we're not allowing others to help us, we need to change. One sided relationships are really not relationships. Looking at the 12th to the 16th verses, shows us it's not the act, but it's the attitude that is important.

GOAL SETTING:

1) Who do you want to bless?

   _____
   _____
   _____
   _____
   _____

2) Who are your priority relationships?

   _____
   _____
   _____
   _____
   _____

3) How often do you want to bless them?

   _____
   _____
   _____
   _____
   _____

4) Where do you want to give (what organizations)?

   _____
   _____
   _____
   _____
   _____

5) What impact do you want to make and through whom?

   _____
   _____
   _____
   _____
   _____

List the gifts you want to give that are outside of your regular tithe (given to your local church). Include short-term goals, long-term goals, and family goals. Don't forget birthdays, offerings and regular gift giving.

_____

_____

_____

_____

_____

_____

_____

Additional Thoughts:

_____

_____

_____

_____

_____

_____

_____

_____

_____

Goals (cont.)

Short Term

Savings _____
_____
_____
_____
_____

Debt Reduction

_____
_____
_____
_____
_____

Long Term

Credit Score

_____
_____
_____ Investing _____
_____ _____
_____
_____
_____

BUDGETING:

1) Set aside a specific dollar amount per month for your giving. Consider the total dollars in the goal setting exercise and divide by 12.
2) Be prepared for those organizations that you contribute to regularly.
3) Decide ahead of time which charitable special requests you will support and at what level. Be careful with emotional giving.
4) Know your budget and delay the giving to the following month if needed.
5) Find an accountability partner, preferably one in the ICE or FIRE category.
6) Consider other ways of contributing to charitable organizations that don't add to your budget.

As an example, Amazon Smile provides an opportunity to contribute to a nonprofit organization based on the amount that you spend. This can be contributed on a regular basis. Additionally, Red Robin heroes allows you to contribute to a specific local school. These examples don't require you to spend any more than you normally would, but you'll be able to contribute to causes you care about. Many companies will allow you to select a portion of your purchase to go toward charitable giving. Save for giving; know what you're planning on giving. Have a goal for the year with your top three causes, or just one. If you don't spend the budgeted amount that month, carry it over or put it in the saving for giving account. Consider a legacy gift to your charitable organization. Saving is important. Make sure you cover your needs first.

'Render unto Caesar the things which are Caesars' – Matthew 22:21

Withholdings	Actual	Budgeted	Notes:
Federal Income Tax			
State Income Tax			
City Income Tax			
FICA			
Medical Insurance			
Dental Insurance			
Vision Insurance			
Health Savings Account (FSA/HSA)			
401(k)			
Total Withholdings			

'Rich rule over the poor and the borrower is slave to the lender' Proverbs 22:7

Finance Payments	Actual	Budgeted	
Credit Card 1			
Credit Card 2			
Credit Card 3			
Credit Card 4			
Student loan			
Auto Loan/ Car Payment			
Home Mortgage			
Personal loan			
Total Finance Payments			

Additional Thoughts:

_____
_____
_____
_____
_____
_____
_____
_____
_____
_____

DEBT REDUCTION:

If you are not debt free; maximize the amount you pay toward bills to eliminate debt.

Once you are debt free,

1) Consider helping your children or other family members by using your giving fund to eliminate their debt.
2) Consider giving to a charitable organization in the name of someone else. This could be a tax deduction for them.

Debt Snowball   The wicked borrow and do not repay – Psalm 37:21

Company	Debt owed	Interest Rate	Term of Loan	Minimum Payment	Amount Paying
1.					
2.					
3.					
4.					
5.					

Additional Thoughts:

_____
_____
_____
_____
_____
_____
_____
_____

CONTEMPLATION:

Sit for a moment and ask God to search your heart. Review the questions, especially in the mindset category. Consider your relationships. Make the necessary adjustments.

Notes:

_____
_____
_____
_____
_____
_____
_____
_____
_____
_____

Ask God to send the right friends, the right partners, and the right relationships and trust that He will.

Additional Thoughts:

_____
_____
_____
_____
_____
_____
_____
_____
_____

LIFE LESSONS:

Remember these things.

1) There will always be worthy causes and people in need.
2) You are simply just one person and you can't meet the needs of everyone.
3) What you offer does make an impact, so do be generous. But it doesn't hurt to ask them to pay it forward.
4) The basic lesson is that we must show compassion to those in need. Even your enemy is supposed to be treated as a neighbor.

5) Loving your neighbor is vitally important, but such sacrifice should not draw attention away from your love for God.
6) Love and devotion for God should not ever be compromised, not even for good deeds.

As a testimony: A friend's ex sister-in-law came into town. There had been no communication for over five years. The ex sister-in-law asked to borrow $2,000 in order to get her car fixed. It is ludicrous that someone with a disconnected relationship would be so audacious. The emotional tug was real but wisdom led to declining the request. A STEAM personality, might be so tempted to help in that situation to bridge a gap in a relationship or to mend a fence.

Beware, similar situations like this occur often; sparkly objects, long lost relatives in need, or a high maintenance friend. Balance emotion with logic.

Final words to contemplate: If you give them a fish sandwich, they'll eat for the day. If you teach them how to fish, they'll eat for a lifetime. It's time to **BLOW OFF SOME STEAM**.

Additional Thoughts:
_____
_____
_____
_____
_____
_____
_____

WATER : Why Attend To Every Report

AVATAR: Wanda the wanderer and Wayne whose name means driver.

Personality: AVOIDER

This personality type is the AVOIDER, but life always catches up with you. If you don't track where your money is going, it tends to get away from you fast. Amassing bills and not keeping detailed records will eventually result in financial instability.

It reminds me of getting out of college and starting that first job. It's when someone else has always taken care of the financial obligations, and now you find yourself trying to figure it out. You forget and that bill gets paid late because you didn't have it written down in your calendar. It's the lack of details, that puts this personality in a position of feeling overwhelmed in some instances, and not being able to truly enjoy life or live financially free.

This personality has some good traits, as well as some others. This might be you if you're thinking 'I owe, I owe so off to work I go'. You may also think you can just get a second job or even a third job temporarily to take care of some of the fun you desire. It's because you're all about fun, enjoying life, and adventure. Usually the second and third job becomes permanent, and that's not a good thing. This WATER category may also believe that as long as there are checks in the checkbook it's okay to write it. Thinking you can just pray very hard, when you swipe your debit card and it'll go through; sometimes works. Eventually, life catches up with you.

One of the biggest issues that really show how bad not paying attention to the details as it relates to money is the pandemic of 2020. We thought life was going to be grand looking forward to 2020. It was going to be the year of clear vision. Everything changed with one little bacteria, and the world shut down. Businesses shut down and families and finances were magnified to see that money management skills were lacking. It didn't have to be the pandemic of 2020, it could simply be a health issue or a diagnosis that completely takes you off kilter. Medical bills can easily exceed income, or a job loss could significantly affect your financial situation. In losing that job, the things you thought you deserved need to be put on hold. Now you're overwhelmed.

The mindset within this personality is that of entitlement. You're absolutely right, you do deserve enjoyment; maybe just not now.

ANIMAL: Ostrich

The animal for the WATER personality is the ostrich. The proverbial 'I'm going to stick my head in the sand, and therefore I don't have to do anything'. As long as I'm not paying attention to the details, eventually everything is going to work out all right. It really doesn't happen that way.

There are some good qualities as well as some warnings for this particular personality. Enjoying life is what Jesus died for us to have. You're supposed to enjoy life, that's a good thing. A heart for adventure, and for others is also a positive. You want others in relationship to share the fun and to have some of the happiness too; that's all great. You're right, you do deserve to enjoy your life.

But the problem is the boundary and the warning that sometimes it can't be right now. It's like the kid that decides after getting the first job that the best car should happen immediately. The one that their parents had and they've always dreamed. Sounds good on the surface but there was no saving or time to earn it. You buy the car, and forget that you have to pay for the insurance which is higher than expected. You have to renew your driver's license, pay registration, and a car tag. It's all those little details that come along with purchases or plans that cost more than anticipated. Details are important.

Another warning is the lack of an accountability partner. Your friends that are along for the ride; they want Mr. Fun or Miss Personality which will take you into ruin. Remember the passage that if we show ourselves friendly, we'll have many friends. The Bible warns us in the book of Proverbs, that if we have a lot of associations, it will bring us to ruin. We want to remember that warning and delay some of the things that we desire. We have to remember that we can't pay for everything. Details are so important, because late fees will add up. In addition to that, as the ostrich puts his head in the sand, kicking the can down the road, spending what is supposed to be for tomorrow, is not good. Retirement means that when we look down the road, without adequate preparation; trouble is inevitable. That's the water personality.

SCRIPTURE LESSON:

The lesson is on The Prodigal Son.

Luke 15:11-24: *"He (Jesus) also said: "A man had two sons. The younger of them said to his father, 'Father, give me the share of the estate I have coming to me.' So he distributed the assets to them. Not many days later, the younger son gathered together all he had and traveled to a distant country, where he squandered his estate in foolish living. After he had spent everything, a severe famine struck that country, and he had nothing. Then he went to work for one of the citizens of that country, who sent him into his fields to feed pigs. He longed to eat his fill from the carob pods the pigs were eating, but no one would give him any. When he came to his senses, he said, 'How many of my father's hired hands have more than enough food, and here I am dying of hunger! I'll get up, go to my father, and say to him, Father, I have sinned against heaven and in your sight. I'm no longer worthy to be called your son. Make me like one of your hired hands.' So he got up and went to his father. But while the son was still a long way off, his father saw him and was filled with compassion. He ran, threw his arms around his neck, and kissed him. The son said to him, 'Father, I have sinned against heaven and in your sight. I'm no longer worthy to be called your son.'* "But the *father told his slaves, 'Quick! Bring out the best robe and put it on him; put a ring on his finger and sandals on his feet. Then bring the fattened calf and slaughter it, and let's celebrate with a feast, because this son of mine was dead and is alive again; he was lost and is found!' So they began to celebrate."*

OBSERVATION:

The word prodigal means frivolous living, and that's what he did. This happens when one is immature before complete understanding. It could continue to occur if one doesn't wake up out of that stupor. That immaturity sometimes leads to making financial decisions that are not necessarily the best; it does eventually catch up.

Additional Thoughts:

_____
_____
_____
_____
_____
_____
_____
_____
_____

BACKGROUND INFORMATION:

Notice the young man said give me what's coming to me. This phrase is stronger than it appears. The word give is in the imperative mood meaning he commanded his father. The entire conversation was very disrespectful; the tone and the fact that inheritance wasn't to be given until after his father's death. He was treating the father as if he were dead. His departure sealed the lack of concern. The request was absolutely premature. He spent money today that was earmarked for the future without regard for the benefactor.

The father gave him his portion of the inheritance. Custom required that the older son receives twice as much as the younger son. The younger son then took 1/3 of the father's entire estate and squandered it. The Bible records that not many days later the many friends and the money that bought them were gone; there was absolutely nothing left. Squander, by definition is to waste something, especially money or time, and do it in a foolish manner. This includes lost opportunities.

The Scripture indicates that there was a famine in the land which magnified the problem. Famine is a period of extreme scarcity of food, meaning that basic needs are no longer being met. The young man began to be in need. Now when he was feeding the pigs and eating their slop, Jewish custom identified pigs as the most detestable animal. For him to be eating the slop that the pigs were eating, and working with them was him reaching his lowest point. He eventually comes to his senses (he comes to himself). He has a revelation.

Repentance happened after he took so much for granted. He had taken for granted his father and what he provided. He began comparing; his old life to his current situation. He came to the conclusion that his father's servants live better than he was currently living. He has an 'AHA' moment. He said to himself, 'I am going to go to my father and ask him to make me one of his servants'. He surmised that he would be much better off as a servant of his father. Repentance occurs after a revelation of the act committed compared to God's standard and a turn toward God's ways. The young man's repentance is evident in that he recognized he had given up his rights as a son. His new request was a humbling of his position and a recognition of his lack of appreciation in the previous interaction. 'Father I have sinned against heaven and in your sight. I am no longer worthy to be called your son.' Usually when repentance occurs there is an understanding and an appreciation of previous circumstances.

Looking at the text again, 'his father saw him and was filled with compassion. He ran'. While the son was rehearsing his humbling speech, the father was moved to run to meet him. Remember the definition of compassion; to alleviate the consequence of sin or suffering in the lives of others. Though the young man sinned and the consequence would have been possible servanthood at best, the father removed the punishment and enthusiastically welcomed him back. Now, this is not normal because fathers didn't run. The father was so overjoyed. This is a representation of our Heavenly Father; He comes to our aid. He's ready when we are ready to repent. He's standing, He's looking, He knows where we are and He wants to bring us back into the fold and celebrate. Notice, the father said the son was dead, and now he's alive; he was lost, and now he is found. That's the way God feels about us. He cares and His compassion moves Him to action.

Other things to highlight include the fathers desire to celebrate as the son returns. He tells his servants to prepare the fatted calf, put a robe on him, and give him a ring. All of that has symbolism; the best robe was a sign of an important position. It showed authority given to the son. The ring, denoted authority as well. The sandals indicated luxury. The fatted calf represented a special occasion.

Turning our attention to verse 25, we see the older son and an understanding of what some of the ramifications might be for this WATER personality. It says, *"Now his older son was in the field; as he came near the house, he heard music and dancing. So he summoned one of the servants and asked what these things meant. 'Your brother is here,' he told him, 'and your father has slaughtered the fattened calf because he has him back safe and sound.'* "*Then he became angry and didn't want to go in. So his father came out and pleaded with him. But he replied to his father, 'Look, I have been slaving many years for you, and I have never disobeyed your orders, yet you never gave me a young goat so I could celebrate with my friends. But when this son of yours came, who has devoured your assets with prostitutes, you slaughtered the fattened calf for him.' "Son,' he said to him, 'you are always with me, and everything I have is yours. But we had to celebrate and rejoice, because this brother of yours was dead and is alive again; he was lost and is found."*

Notice the older brother harbored bitterness and was very upset with the destructive ways and the frivolous spending of his younger brother. He saw the waste. Those that watch this WATER personality, are a little disgusted by the spending because they are responsible. In many cases the responsible person watches the irresponsible being rewarded for their behavior; funds to pay off their debt, being absolved of the wasteful practices. Bitterness is a result of doing the right thing and not being acknowledged for the good decisions; an attitude of overlooking and assumption that they don't need. 'Look, I have been slaving many years for you, and I have never disobeyed your orders, yet you never gave me a young goat so I could celebrate with my friends.' gets the short end of the stick. The father wanted both sons to celebrate and the reason given was that the younger son was lost but now he's found.

A few other things to point out. For those on the outside looking in at the one that is squandering, they are making judgments. The responsible person is embittered, and seems to be punished for taking care of business, while the reckless seem to have all the enjoyment. This may cause others to not want to be around or deal with you, or loan you any money. Typically, you might avoid trying to pay them back, and they need their money too; it's just as valuable to them. You might avoid paying the bills that you need to pay. Remember what you sow with others you are going to reap. So when they see your reckless behavior, they're expecting that you'll be reckless with them as well.

Additional Thoughts:

_____

_____

_____

_____

_____

_____

_____

_____

INTERPRETATION:

Tips from the Scripture: Keep in mind he was young and immature though this behavior can happen at any age.

1) Unwise decisions, especially financial ones, can lead to loss of opportunity, as well as loss of friendships. Friends that are with you only when you have money and leave you afterwards, aren't true friends.
2) Prodigal living can lead to unwise decisions at any age.
3) Not appreciating what you have, can lead to losing out on great relationships, as well as very good opportunities.
4) Spending money that is earmarked for your future, in today's day and age, leads to trouble later on, and possibly will lead to loss.
5) Repentance is necessary regardless of your past. Our Heavenly Father is standing ready to receive you back and to intervene into any and every situation. Repentance is required to get back on the right track.
6) The compassion of the Father, regardless of what unwise decisions were made, is ready to restore you 100%.
7) Others see frivolous living and squandering of money and often resent it.
8) Financial irresponsibility often puts a damper on relationships and sometimes that bridge cannot be crossed again.
9) Comparison can result in bitterness and the loss of joy.

Additional Thoughts:

_____
_____
_____
_____
_____
_____
_____
_____
_____

APPLICATION:

There are positives and warnings for this personality just like the others.

Accentuate these areas:

1. Recognize and repent from previous bad financial decisions. A true heart of repentance is necessary including restitution, if possible.
2. Appreciation and gratitude. Take stock of what you currently have, journal if you need to, include key relationships. Learn to appreciate and be grateful for all your blessings.

3. Enjoyment of life; that's what God wants for us. It just might need to be delayed.

Things to eliminate:

1) Only focusing on the present. Start looking to the future and making adequate preparation.
2) The lack of appreciation.
3) The lack of documentation. Make sure that you have adequate records in order to move forward.
4) Debt and the frivolous spending must stop. Set boundaries and don't overspend.
5) Paying your bills randomly needs to cease. Get you on track and automate as much as possible. This will allow your bills to be paid without late fees and your credit score will go up.
6) Late payment fees definitely must be eliminated. This is true for any personality, but especially WATER.

Additional Thoughts:

_____
_____
_____
_____
_____
_____
_____
_____

MINDSET:

Questions to consider:

1) Are you being self-centered? You're doing all the enjoyment without taking responsibility.

   _____
   _____
   _____
   _____
   _____

2) Do you have the 'you only live once (YOLO)' mindset?

   _____
   _____
   _____
   _____
   _____

3) Do you think you will always be in debt, so why be concerned? Well, that's not the case. You don't always have to be in debt. Live for today and also save to live comfortably tomorrow.

_____

_____

_____

_____

_____

4) Do you know the difference between luxuries and necessities? Make sure that you remove the fear of missing out (FOMO). God said that He did not give us a spirit of fear, but of love, power and a sound mind.

_____

_____

_____

_____

_____

5) Is it within your budget? Yes, enjoy life, but it still needs to be within your budget.

_____
_____
_____
_____
_____

Your key is to prioritize, plan and prepare.

Additional Thoughts:
_____
_____
_____
_____
_____
_____
_____
_____
_____

GOAL SETTING:

1. Concentrate on long-term goals then work backwards into the short-term goal. That way you will know what you need every single month.
2. Make preparation a priority.
3. An emergency fund is necessary for you, as well as 9 months of gross income. If you lose your job, you won't be up at night stressing and worrying. You'll have the time that's necessary to find another one.
4. Get on track with paying your bills. Automation would be ideal.
5. Check for missing money, unclaimed property and unclaimed assets. Use these funds to jumpstart your savings and emergency fund. www.usa.gov www.unclaimed.org www.missingmoney.com www.fiscal.treasury.gov

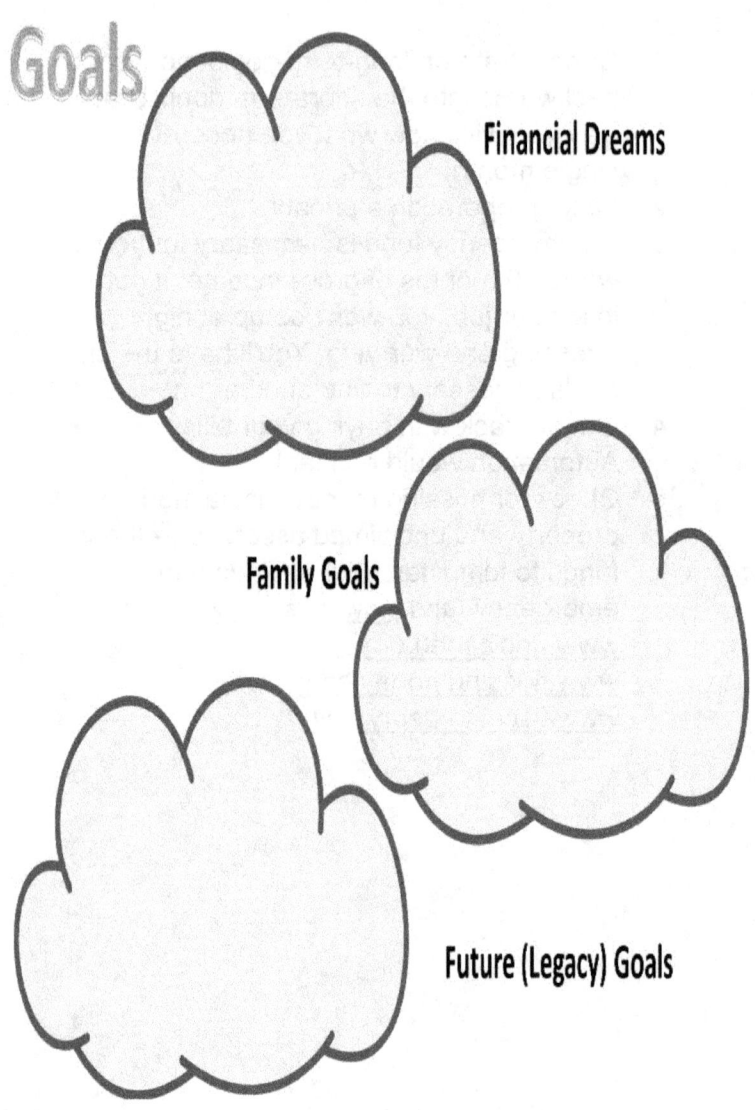

Goals (cont.)

Short Term

Savings _____
_____
_____
_____

Debt Reduction _____
_____
_____
_____
_____

Credit Score

Long Term _____
_____
_____
_____

Investing _____
_____
_____
_____

Additional Thoughts:

_____
_____
_____
_____
_____
_____
_____
_____
_____
_____

BUDGETING:

1. You've got to create a budget. For you especially, a balanced budget is necessary. Determine how much you have coming in, and how much you have going out. Work within 80% of your income. Why? Because 10% you're going to save and 10% you're going to give (tithe). You're going to adequately prepare.
2. Get an accountability partner, preferably someone on the ICE or the FIRE categories, because you don't want someone that's a spender just like you.

3. Get a clear understanding of where you are.
    a. Know your financial payments (minimum requirement).
    b. Know your debts (full balance owed and the percent interest). This can be a rude awakening but don't despair. Making great financial decisions now will eventually improve financial status.
4. Don't be emotional about what you're missing. Yes, you'll get a chance to enjoy a little bit later. Planning is the key, as well as debt reduction.
5. Don't be so free to spend, every dollar should count and should be in a specific category. Keep them there.
6. Journal your spending, that way, you'll have a clear understanding of where you're spending your money and you can make the appropriate decisions.
7. Evaluate every single line item on your budget to find out what you can eliminate, what you can cut back on, and what should stay.

'Render unto Caesar the things which are Caesars' – Matthew 22:21

Withholdings	Actual	Budgeted	Notes:
Federal Income Tax			
State Income Tax			
City Income Tax			
FICA			
Medical Insurance			
Dental Insurance			
Vision Insurance			
Health Savings Account (FSA/HSA)			
401(k)			
Total Withholdings			

'Rich rule over the poor and the borrower is slave to the lender' Proverbs 22:7

Finance Payments	Actual	Budgeted
Credit Card 1		
Credit Card 2		
Credit Card 3		
Credit Card 4		
Student loan		
Auto Loan/ Car Payment		
Home Mortgage		
Personal loan		
Total Finance Payments		

Additional Thoughts:

_____
_____
_____
_____
_____
_____
_____
_____
_____
_____

SAVING:

1. Set up automatic savings (10% going directly into your savings account). Pay yourself before you pay your bills.
2. Set up your emergency fund. Sell things you are no longer utilizing. This can be a treasure for someone else and add money to your pocket. It's a great way to start your emergency fund of the first $1,000.

Additional Thoughts:

_____
_____
_____
_____
_____
_____
_____
_____

I'm including a 52 week savings challenge which can be done to stimulate your saving. If you find it difficult initially to balance your budget by including 10% savings, use a lower percentage and pair it with this challenge. You can use the savings bingo as another option. Automatically deposit as great a percentage as possible into your savings account regularly.

52 Week Money Challenge

Week	Deposit Amount	Account Balance	Week	Deposit Amount	Account Balance
1	1.00	$1.00	27	27.00	$378.00
2	2.00	$3.00	28	28.00	$406.00
3	3.00	$6.00	29	29.00	$435.00
4	4.00	$10.00	30	30.00	$465.00
5	5.00	$15.00	31	31.00	$496.00
6	6.00	$21.00	32	32.00	$528.00
7	7.00	$28.00	33	33.00	$561.00
8	8.00	$36.00	34	34.00	$595.00
9	9.00	$45.00	35	35.00	$630.00
10	10.00	$55.00	36	36.00	$666.00
11	11.00	$66.00	37	37.00	$703.00
12	12.00	$78.00	38	38.00	$741.00
13	13.00	$91.00	39	39.00	$780.00
14	14.00	$105.00	40	40.00	$820.00
15	15.00	$120.00	41	41.00	$861.00
16	16.00	$136.00	42	42.00	$903.00
17	17.00	$153.00	43	43.00	$946.00
18	18.00	$171.00	44	44.00	$990.00
19	19.00	$190.00	45	45.00	$1,035.00
20	20.00	$210.00	46	46.00	$1,081.00
21	21.00	$231.00	47	47.00	$1,128.00
22	22.00	$253.00	48	48.00	$1,176.00
23	23.00	$276.00	49	49.00	$1,225.00
24	24.00	$300.00	50	50.00	$1,275.00
25	25.00	$325.00	51	51.00	$1,326.00
26	26.00	$351.00	52	52.00	$1,378.00

Savings bingo instructions:

Though you can follow the table each week for the year, I suggest you use it like bingo and put in the maximum you have that week. For instance, though it may be the 1st week of the year but you received an unexpected gift of $50 then put in the $50 and mark that week as complete. If you have enough to cover more than one of the weeks at the higher level, then do so. This means with interest you can save more. This also allows you to work backwards and when the end of the year comes you won't feel strapped about saving $52 that week, instead you will only need $1. The options are many: start at $1 and each week save the designated amount; begin at the end of the chart and work backwards; or use the chart like bingo and deposit the maximum you have available. Either way at the end of the year you have an emergency fund and the beginning of an established savings account.

FREE	29	32	16	4	24	18	8	31
9	43	5	23	38	7	1	41	3
42	15	27	52	47	49	28	22	34
25	37	19	46	FREE	45	26	19	29
11	13	35	50	48	51	14	44	2
33	39	21	39	17	12	36	6	40

DEBT REDUCTION:

Go to https://www.vertex42.com/Calculators/debt-reduction-calculator.html it is a debt reduction calculator. You'll need your budget, amount you owe on credit card payments, student loans, and the mortgage. You will need to know the full balance as well as the interest you're paying. Based on the amount of money you identify to pay down debt, it will calculate when you will be debt free. Concentrate on clearing all of your debt. The majority of whatever is leftover should be going toward debt reduction.

Debt Snowball   The wicked borrow and do not repay – Psalm 37:21

Company	Debt owed	Interest Rate	Term of Loan	Minimum Payment	Amount Paying
1.					
2.					
3.					
4.					
5.					

Additional Thoughts:

_____
_____
_____
_____
_____
_____
_____
_____
_____

CREDIT:

Because you are adversely affecting your score, this section is important. Payment history (number of late payments), debt owed, percent utilization and derogatory marks all go into determining your credit score. Your low score is a function of how you've handled your payments.

1. Set up automatic payments for most of your bills. Why? Because when you're paying your bills on time, over time your credit score will go up.

2. Take an assessment of your current credit score. www.freecreditreport.com You can get a free credit report once per year. Make sure you know exactly what is on your report and your score. Look at all negative items and eliminate them. Have a plan so that they will no longer be on your record.

Credit Score Highlight &Goals

	Goal
• Payment History: # of late payments ____	0
• Amount owed: _____ (this is your total debt)	$0
• % Utilization: _____ (Amount owed/Total limit x 100%)	0%
• Length of credit history: _____ (how long you have had credit)	The longer the better
• Derogatory marks: _____ Date to remove: _____	0
• Current Score _____	700+

Additional Thoughts:

_____
_____
_____
_____
_____
_____
_____
_____

CONTEMPLATION:

Here are some questions to consider:

1) Why do you not pay closer attention to the details?

_____
_____
_____
_____
_____

2) What do you fear?

   _____
   _____
   _____
   _____
   _____

3) What are you avoiding?

   _____
   _____
   _____
   _____
   _____

4) What are some of your actions that require you to repent?

   _____
   _____
   _____
   _____
   _____

5) What Scripture will keep you focused on your goal?

_____
_____
_____
_____
_____

Ask God for guidance and more focus, especially as it relates to your finances.

Additional Thoughts:

_____
_____
_____
_____
_____
_____
_____
_____
_____
_____

LIFE LESSONS:

God does want you to enjoy life, but not to the detriment of your future. Remember, 'A good man leaves an inheritance for his children's children' (Proverbs 13:22). This includes a good woman. God is such a loving father; once you repent, He is willing to restore you 100% (1 John 1:9). Past mistakes do not determine your future benefits and blessings. Look out for miracles and be grateful for all the blessings you continue to receive.

Your fun-loving spirit is an asset, add boundaries to stay on the narrow path that leads to life (Matthew 7:14). Being wise and counting the cost is extremely important. Build on a sure foundation (Luke 14:28).

Here's the best testimony: A WATER personality client had been paying bills, but didn't keep good records. There was a legal judgment against her to pay the bill again because she could not prove payment. She had several consistently late payments and additional fees were assessed. Her mindset was that she would always be in debt; she thought it was a way of life. However, the Bible says, 'Owe no man but to love him' (Romans 13:8). After her wisdom wealth workshop, her attitude was different; she was on a fixed income but she saw light at the end of the tunnel. Her entire budget was balanced; including fun, giving, saving, and spending. Debt reduction was one of her priorities and it too was included within her budget. She was overpaying and had overpaid her utility bill, this was refunded and fully funded her emergency account ($1,000). Automatic savings were set up positioning her to become an automatic millionaire. She is confident and financially educated. She has a budget; she knows her expenses including the allocation for fun and she works within the boundaries. In addition, her debt reduction plan gave her hope. Using the debt calculator, overdraft fees, legal fees, mortgage and her student loan will be completely paid off within six years. Her response, 'I am mad happy, it is something that everybody should have'.

You too can have financial freedom; you'll just have to **CONTAIN THE WATER**.

Additional Thoughts:

_____
_____
_____
_____
_____
_____
_____
_____
_____

ICE: I Can't Entertain

Avatar: Iris, the rainbow catcher, who strategically plans for the future. Isaac who looks ahead and laughs because he has planned for the future.

Personality: SAVER

ICE stands for I Can't Entertain. As one who pays close attention to money management details, this personality is a natural fit. In growing up, we didn't have a whole lot. We didn't know that we were missing anything but we didn't spend on unnecessary items. I always paid attention to every little single penny. In college, I was the coupon queen. I would cut out the coupons and send them to my mom so she could save money on groceries. Sally (sale) and Clarissa (clearance) were my best friends. If it wasn't on clearance, I didn't buy it. If it wasn't discounted; it wasn't for me and I was going to wait. We should make great financial decisions; but if there's a significant positive desire, you shouldn't deny yourself. After all, Jesus died for us to have an enjoyable life.

With the ICE personality, one caution is to remove the scarcity or poverty mindset. From a heart of wanting to help others, I began writing personal finance books.

ANIMAL: Mosquito

The animal for the ICE personality is the mosquito; that blood sucker. He's going to get every little drop of blood out of you. What happens with a mosquito? It leaves a big mark and it's a little itchy, right?

One of the warnings that goes along with the ICE personality is bitterness because the rest of the world, other people, your family and your friends are enjoying life, and you're not. I'm sure you don't want to be bitter.

The good thing with the ICE personality is that you master money management. You're also future focused and a planner. You've got to let go of the calculator and constant reminders to figure everything out. You're probably losing sleep at night, wondering how you're going to pay that next bill, especially if it was unexpected.

Your goal is to add margin (an amount included so as to be sure of success or safety) into your life

SCRIPTURE LESSON:

Luke 12: 13-34 "*Someone from the crowd said to Him, "Teacher, tell my brother to divide the inheritance with me." "Friend," He said to him, "who appointed Me a judge or arbitrator over you?" He then told them, "Watch out and be on guard against all greed because one's life is not in the abundance of his possessions." Then He told them a parable: "A rich man's land was very productive. He thought to himself, 'What should I do, since I don't have anywhere to store my crops? I will do this,' he said. 'I'll tear down my barns and build bigger ones and store all my grain and my goods there. Then I'll say to myself, "You have many goods stored up for many years. Take it easy; eat, drink, and enjoy yourself.'" "But God said to him, 'You fool! This very night your life is demanded of you. And the things you have prepared—whose will they be?' "That's how it is with the one who stores up treasure for himself and is not rich toward God." Then He said to His disciples: "Therefore I tell you, don't worry about your life, what you will eat; or about the body, what you will wear. For life is more than food and the body more than clothing. Consider the ravens: They don't sow or reap; they don't have a storeroom or a barn; yet God feeds them. Aren't you worth much more than the birds? Can any of you add a cubit to his height by worrying? If then you're not able to do even a little thing, why worry about the rest? "Consider how the wildflowers grow: They don't labor or spin thread. Yet I tell you, not even Solomon in all his splendor was adorned like one of these! If that's how God clothes the grass, which is in the field today and is thrown into the furnace tomorrow, how much more will He do for you—you of little faith? Don't keep striving for what you should eat and what you should drink, and don't be anxious. For the Gentile world eagerly seeks all these things, and your Father knows that you need them. "But seek His kingdom, and these things will be provided for you. Don't be afraid, little flock, because your Father delights to give you the kingdom. Sell your possessions and give to the poor. Make money-bags for yourselves that won't grow old, an inexhaustible treasure in heaven, where no thief comes near and no moth destroys. For where your treasure is, there your heart will be also."*

OBSERVATION:

Things to consider:
1. Verse 13 says watch out for greed; that's self-centered desire for possessions and wealth. His land is productive; this man was doing well! Productive indicates that he was able to produce large amounts of goods, commodities or results. He asked himself; notice he didn't ask anyone else. He turned his thoughts inward. He thought he knew it all and asked himself what he should do.
2. Planning is good, but remember tomorrow isn't promised. If we continue to plan for tomorrow and when it arrives or if it doesn't, what will we have?
3. God calls him a fool. Fool is the word morros where we get our English word moron. A moron is a person that's lacking in judgment or prudence. It's one that's lacking in common powers of understanding. It's also one that is marked with a propensity for fondness for something. This can lead you down the road to addiction because you desire the shiny object. God calls this a misappropriation of priorities, and He calls it foolish.
4. 'The things that you've prepared whose are they going to be?' (asked in verse 20b) Yes, we're supposed to leave an inheritance for our children's children but we're also to enjoy life while we're here on earth. Don't wait to the fourth quarter of your life to start

enjoying. When three quarters have gone by, you may not be able to redeem the time.
5. Don't neglect the spiritual side for material gain. We must be rich toward God is the ultimate message. We have to put the spiritual over the material. The order is God, family, and then ministry. We are to enjoy. You are worth more than you give yourself credit! So, value your contributions.
6. Worrying is very unproductive; it's like sitting in a rocking chair going back and forth. You do a whole lot of work, putting in a lot of effort, but getting nowhere. Mentally calculating over and over does not accomplish anything either. It's just like a rocking chair.
7. Increase your faith! God asked whose is it going to be? Are you really trusting in the riches? Or are you trusting in God? Put your trust in God! When the Scripture records that the man was striving, the definition is to make great efforts to achieve or attain something. God said you're striving for these things and you're anxious. Anxious reflects that you're experiencing worry, unease as well as nervousness regarding an outcome. Your Father knows what you're in need of before you even ask. He says seek the Kingdom first and everything else will be added.

Ultimately, the question is where is your heart? The Bible says that where your treasure is, there your heart will be also. A quick way of answering is to check your checkbook. Where are you spending your money? There you'll find your number one priority.

Additional Thoughts:

_____
_____
_____
_____
_____
_____
_____
_____
_____

INTERPRETATION:

1. Material gain should not take precedence over the spiritual investment. Your heart is connected to your wallet.
2. Watch out for greed. Greed does tend to escalate with the accumulation of possessions.
3. The attitude of anxiety is destructive to your physical life and hurtful to your spiritual testimony. Using your energy to worry over things that you cannot control is futile.

God sees, He knows, and He provides.

Additional Thoughts:

_____
_____
_____
_____
_____
_____
_____
_____
_____

APPLICATION:

1. You are doing great staying on track. Continue to do that!
2. Continue budgeting and living within your means.
3. Continue planning for the future.

Those are great and should be accentuated just add some enjoyment for today into your budget.

Eliminate worrying and constant recalculating. Put those things to bed.

Additional Thoughts:

_____
_____
_____
_____
_____
_____
_____
_____
_____

MINDSET:

This can be the know-it-all personality; you think you have it all figured out or you're the only one that can. Always remain teachable because there are other options that are available. Be open to the blessings and the miracles that may come.

The desperate mindset can also rise here because you are always calculating to the very penny. The key is to seek God first before you seek the calculator. One of the big questions to ponder is, why do you deprive yourself? See yourself through the eyes of the cross and see that you are worthy, loved, fun and enjoyable. God created you and He created you to enjoy like everyone else.

Additional Thoughts:

_____
_____
_____
_____
_____
_____
_____
_____
_____

GOAL SETTING:

"Eat the Cookie, Buy the Shoes" ~ Joyce Meyer

1. Simply put, you need to learn to enjoy and celebrate, even in small bites. Whatever and wherever it may be because you are working hard. You are doing so many things. You are being extremely responsible. All of that is great but you need to celebrate a little for yourself as well.
2. Set a goal! Identify a short-term goal that you can achieve that's going to be enjoyment for you. Don't forget what you enjoy doing and what you would like to do. Bake it into the plan and start living.

Additional Thoughts:

_____
_____
_____
_____
_____
_____
_____
_____
_____

Goals

Financial Dreams

Family Goals

Future (Legacy) Goals

Goals (cont.)

Savings

Debt Reduction

Short Term

Long Term

Credit Score

Investing

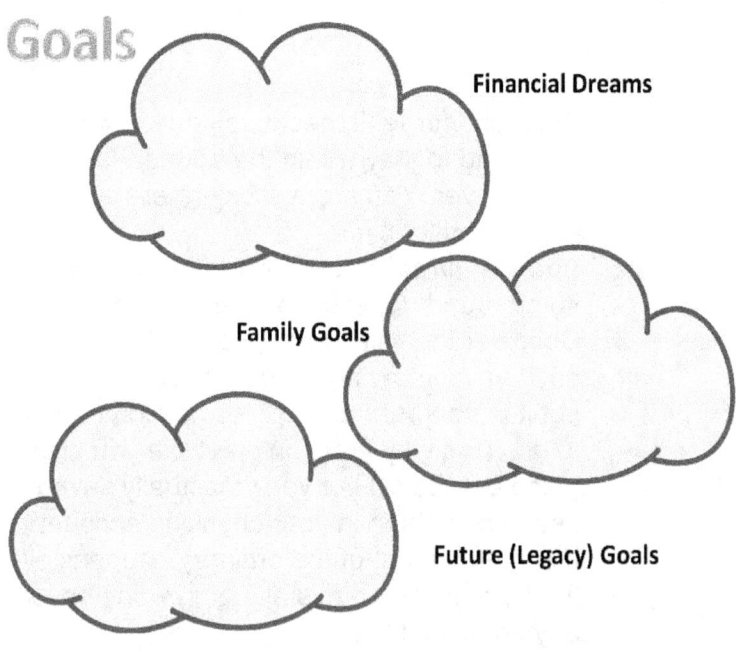

BUDGETING:

1. Set it and forget it, because you know you are going to stay within the boundaries. You are a saver. You are a stickler here so go ahead and let it ride.
2. Add margin so that you don't feel pressured. If you round up, you won't feel so bound.
3. Consider the sale items (the savings) and put it in your savings account. Specifically, put it in your fun account, something for you to do. That way you don't feel like you are going overboard but you've actually saved.
4. Leave a cushion in your checking account. If something out of the ordinary happens or the bank makes a mistake, you won't have any additional fees.
5. Automate your bills as much as possible. This will remove the constant attention and calculation.

Additional Thoughts:

_____
_____
_____
_____
_____
_____
_____

'Render unto Caesar the things which are Caesars' – Matthew 22:21

Withholdings	Actual	Budgeted	Notes:
Federal Income Tax			
State Income Tax			
City Income Tax			
FICA			
Medical Insurance			
Dental Insurance			
Vision Insurance			
Health Savings Account (FSA/HSA)			
401(k)			

Total Withholdings

'Rich rule over the poor and the borrower is slave to the lender' Proverbs 22:7

Finance Payments	Actual	Budgeted
Credit Card 1		
Credit Card 2		
Credit Card 3		
Credit Card 4		
Student loan		
Auto Loan/ Car Payment		
Home Mortgage		
Personal loan		

Total Finance Payments

SAVING:

1. When making short-term and long-term goals, use percentages. As you continue to make more money and have more income, your savings will also increase. You can be an automatic millionaire because you plan ahead and stick to your budget.
2. Pay yourself before you pay your bills.

Additional Thoughts:

_____
_____
_____
_____
_____
_____
_____
_____

DEBT REDUCTION:

1. Normally for you, debt is not a big issue. If it is, you already have a plan in order to pay it off. If debt is your biggest concern then devise a plan. Make sure you go to this website: https://www.vertex42.com/Calculators/debt-reduction-calculator.html Identify your financial freedom date. Once you do this, make sure that you stay debt free.
2. Set up your bills to automatically include your debt payments.

Debt Snowball   The wicked borrow and do not repay – Psalm 37:21

Company	Debt owed	Interest Rate	Term of Loan	Minimum Payment	Amount Paying
1.					
2.					
3.					
4.					
5.					

Additional Thoughts:

_____
_____
_____
_____
_____
_____
_____
_____
_____

CONTEMPLATION:

Here are some questions to consider:

1) Are you acknowledging God in your finances?

_____
_____
_____
_____
_____

2) What does God have the ability to do in your life?

   _____
   _____
   _____
   _____
   _____

3) Do you trust God completely?

   _____
   _____
   _____
   _____
   _____

4) What areas are you holding onto a sense of control?

   _____
   _____
   _____
   _____
   _____

5) How do you feel about your future?

_____
_____
_____
_____

6) Did you grow up with a poverty/scarcity mindset?

_____
_____
_____
_____

7) When did you develop a scarcity mindset?

_____
_____
_____
_____

8) What Scriptures should you study/memorize to break the cycle of thoughts of lack?

_____
_____
_____
_____
_____

9) Where do you feel incomplete?

_____
_____
_____
_____
_____

10) Why don't you feel you deserve to enjoy life?

_____
_____
_____
_____
_____

11) What does enjoyment look like for you?

_____
_____
_____
_____
_____

12) Who hurt you that you need to release?

_____
_____
_____
_____
_____

13) Are you harboring bitterness? Why?

_____
_____
_____
_____
_____

14) Are you holding onto unforgiveness?

_____
_____
_____
_____
_____

15) Who are you not valuing?

_____
_____
_____
_____
_____

16) Gratitude is important! What would you add to a gratitude list today?

_____
_____
_____
_____
_____

17) What would you like God to change in your life?

_____

_____

_____

_____

_____

18) Where can you add margin in your life? What needs to be removed?

_____

_____

_____

_____

_____

19) What activities do you need to add to your schedule to build your spiritual muscle?

_____

_____

_____

_____

_____

20) Where can you stop striving and trust God?

_____
_____
_____
_____
_____

Additional Thoughts:

_____
_____
_____
_____
_____
_____
_____
_____
_____
_____

LIFE LESSONS:

All work and no play makes Jack a dull boy, it does the same for Jane. It causes resentment and bitterness if it's not checked. Don't be like the older brother in the Luke 15 passage, not enjoying the party because you are paying too much attention to the details. Celebrate life! Find areas of fun that you can enjoy and add them to your budget. Whether it's just $5 a week for a movie or a smoothie; something that you do for yourself. That small celebration is going to eliminate a lifetime of resentment.

Another admonition: if you don't fill yourself up first, you're not going to have much to fill others. That is what this personality is all about. You are so 'other centered' that you are not taking care of you. Do you recall the instructions at the beginning of flight? Should the mask fall from the overhead, in order to help others, you need to first place your mask over your face. You have to be filled first.

Finally, let me end with my testimony. I was going through life doing so much for my entire family, making sure everybody had everything they needed. I was the coupon queen. Sally and Clarissa were my best friends. I wasn't buying or doing much for myself. I began doing what I'm telling you to do. I added in going to the movies once a week (discounted to $5 on Tuesdays). I had an opportunity to enjoy. In addition, I sometimes added in a smoothie and scheduled a monthly massage. I started paying myself first and putting my savings away before I started paying my bills. Yes, that meant cutting back on some of the bills but it allowed me to enjoy. I recognized that I already planned for my future but now I planned for some fun. If that resonates with you, I want you to jump on board too. If you are an ICE personality, I Can't Entertain, I need you to **MELT THE ICE**. Enjoy with the rest of your family and friends.

Additional Thoughts:

_____
_____
_____
_____
_____
_____
_____
_____
_____

FIRE: Financially Independent Retiring Early

Avatar: Felecia meaning happy and Frank a free man.

This position is the desired goal. Little Chonta was not at the FIRE position. Yes, I was always taught to save and I started early. On my first corporate job, I made $25,000 per year. I began investing in a 401K that was offered with my company. They matched my contributions up to a percentage allowing me to double my investment immediately. Starting at an early age (20) investing was a good financial decision. I continued the strategic financial moves by renting for only one year. I then purchased a townhouse. The amount of money I was spending on the townhouse for my mortgage was just slightly more than the rent of the apartment. I also realized I was building equity in my own property and not continuing to pay for someone else's. These were wise decisions. Not having an entrepreneurial spirit from the beginning is where I could have improved. I thought that as long as I continued to work making and saving a lot of money, I would be in a great position. This was good. A better position would be to own your own business or intellectual property. This allows you to have something that makes money while you sleep. Again, you want to be SWISS; making Sales While I Sleep Soundly. That is extreme investment and that is when you are really on FIRE. You don't want it to just kindled a little, you want it to burn brightly.

Personality: SECURITY

This personality is one of security; always prepared and always positioned for the future. Looking forward but also enjoying life today. It is to be pursued and desired and it is great to be in this position.

ANIMAL: Ant

The animal associated with this personality is the ant. In the Proverbs it talks about the ant. 'Look to the ant you sluggard' (Proverbs 6:6-11). Ants build colonies and make ant hills. You visibly see where they have built. If you run over an ant hill as you cut the grass, you would think that it would be abolished. The foundation runs extremely deep and they are prepared for adverse conditions and before long that ant hill is right back where it started.

You've done some of the same things if you are in the FIRE category, preparation has been made for adverse or harsh conditions. You also recognize that enjoying life is possible and necessary. You are living life to the fullest but you've also prepared for the future. You have your budgeting down. An accountability partner may not be necessary but you might have a financial advisor to make sure that you are diversifying. You are also reaching out to others, extending that olive branch to pull them up, to teach what you have learned. Whether you learned it the hard way by finding your own financial literacy or you had a mentor. You are willing to help others because you set your goals to include assisting others to reach your level.

Often you are a target so be warned, don't throw your pearls before swine. In other words, don't give all of your wisdom to an opportunist trying to take advantage. You need to put boundaries in place; stop gap measures that would ensure your protection. If they burn you once then they won't burn you twice.

I applaud you for reaching this FIRE category! It is attainable. We are studying the Scripture, learning and preparing so that when you reach this level you can help somebody else IGNITE THE FIRE.

Wisdom is also associated with the FIRE category. Not only are you watchful over what you have, but you look out for great opportunities. You are also watchful for other people. In addition, you are intentional about your investments. You make alliances and partnerships that maximize your profit.

You also speak life. You speak into others. You don't keep quiet about what you've gone through or what you know. You reach back to help others. You are determined; determined that you are prepared for the future should any adverse circumstance arise you evaluate and engineer a plan to succeed. You look for opportunities; they abound in every situation. You are always on guard and ready to pounce on any opportunity that is appropriate.

You are merciful to those less fortunate and those who lacked opportunity. You are willing to reach out to the poor and to give to the needy.

So when you think about being watchful, intentional, speaking out, being determined, looking for opportunities and being merciful, it all amounts to wisdom.

Go ahead and **IGNITE THE FIRE**

SCRIPTURE LESSON:

Proverbs 31:10-31 (The Proverbs 31 woman):
"Who can find a capable wife? She is far more precious than jewels. The heart of her husband trusts in her, and he will not lack anything good. She rewards him with good, not evil, all the days of her life. She selects wool and flax and works with willing hands. She is like the merchant ships, bringing her food from far away. She rises while it is still night and provides food for her household and portions for her female servants. She evaluates a field and buys it; she plants a vineyard with her earnings. She draws on her strength and reveals that her arms are strong. She sees that her profits are good, and her lamp never goes out at night. She extends her hands to the spinning staff, and her hands hold the spindle. Her hands reach out to the poor, and she extends her hands to the needy. She is not afraid for her household when it snows, for all in her household are doubly clothed. She makes her own bed coverings; her clothing is fine linen and purple. Her husband is known at the city gates, where he sits among the elders of the land. She makes and sells linen garments; she delivers belts to the merchants. Strength and honor are her

clothing, and she can laugh at the time to come. She opens her mouth with wisdom and loving instruction is on her tongue. She watches over the activities of her household and is never idle. Her sons rise up and call her blessed. Her husband also praises her: "Many women are capable, but you surpass them all!" Charm is deceptive and beauty is fleeting, but a woman who fears the LORD will be praised. Give her the reward of her labor, and let her works praise her at the city gates."

OBSERVATION:

There is so much to observe and a goal to pursue.

1. She works with her hands willingly; she is not idle. She is not only a willing worker but the impression is one of excellence and giving her extreme best. One of my favorite passages is Colossians 3:23, "Whatever you do, do it with all of your heart, as unto the Lord and not to man." This woman embodies this passage. She doesn't sit back or become lazy.
2. She also provides. 'She provides food for her household and portions for her female servants.' She is always giving and making sure that there are enough provisions. She doesn't slack nor is cheap yet she's not overly extended like the STEAM personality. She's also not like the ICE personality, but has an excellent balance.

3. She evaluates. 'She evaluates a field and buys it.' She's always looking for an opportunity and when she finds an excellent one she jumps on it.
4. She plants (sows) which leads to reaping a harvest. She invests (sows) and she pays attention to those investments. She understands the long game but doesn't worry daily about the fluctuations. She continually invests and evaluates where her funds are placed.
5. She reaches and extends her hand to the poor and the needy. She is merciful, watchful and considerate of the fact that she is in a better position than others. She takes the opportunity to help those who are less fortunate.
6. She's prepared for unfavorable circumstances. 'She is not afraid for her household when it snows for all of her household is doubly clothed.' Notice that not only is she prepared for what they would need right then, but she has extra just in case. In case there is more famine or drought; she is also prepared.
7. She makes, sells and delivers. She has an entrepreneurial spirit. When working for time, your time equals your money; dollars per hour means you have to put in hours to get dollars. If you invent or create something it can work while you are sleeping. You can be SWISS.

8. She is also confident knowing she is adequately prepared. She speaks wisdom, showing others how to achieve what she has amassed. She doesn't take it for granted that they know, she's willing to teach.
9. She's watchful and she's never idle. Idleness is not in her.
10. She fears the Lord! This is probably the greatest area. Her trust is in the Lord, and He favors her. As we look at this woman, her foundation is her fear of the Lord. It doesn't mean that she is afraid of God. It means that she has a reverential fear. She is in awe of who He is; she trusts in Him. She deliberately commits her life, her mind, her heart and her emotions to learning about Him and what He expects of her. As a woman who fears the Lord, she has devoted herself to Him and His ways with a wholehearted pursuit in pleasing Him. Her entire life starts with Him and she listens to Him and she then acts upon everything that she has heard.
11. We find that this woman is also favored by man. Her household calls her blessed and they reward her for her wisdom by singing her praises. She takes care of so many.

For the men reading this, it's for you too. The Proverbs 31 woman is the height of exceptionality and excellence which is where you should aspire. We can also look at Joseph in Genesis chapters 30 through 43. Joseph also had a God-fearing spirit.

He began by wanting to please God and he got not only favor with God but with man. Whatever he put his hands to, it prospered. Others noticed it, so they promoted him. Joseph knew when the famine was coming and he adequately prepared the grain.

Another example is Solomon when he had the opportunity to ask for anything of the Lord. He could have asked for riches and wealth but he asked for wisdom. We need to seek wisdom, God's wisdom. Seeking God's wisdom is the key and all these things will be added.

Additional Thoughts:

_____
_____
_____
_____
_____
_____
_____
_____
_____
_____

INTERPRETATION:

This individual has her priorities in order. The order is God, family then ministry. God first! Fear the Lord which was highlighted. She took care of her family, her household; she blessed others by her wisdom. She took care of others; this is the ministry side. She had the order in its proper place.

Keys to remember:
1. She shops for the best quality. Don't get something cheap because it will need to be replaced quickly. If you buy something of high quality it will last almost a lifetime.
2. She ensures that her family does not run out of supplies. She prepares ahead; her pantry is stocked and she is ready for adverse conditions.
3. She invests her money and works to profit from her investments. The goal of investing is not just to save that nest egg but for it to continue to grow and to leave a legacy. The Bible says that a good man (or woman) leaves an inheritance for his (her) children's children. There are provisions made for family.
4. She helps those that are in need. She is merciful. She has a giving heart unlike the ICE personality who is frugal. She is more giving because she recognizes that she is secure.

Pursue the highest standard of excellence and make sure you prioritize God, family and ministry. Be intentional. Shop for the best qualities. Ensure your family has all their needs met. Prepare ahead for any harsh conditions. Invest and profit from your investments. Meet the needs of those that are less fortunate and be watchful. Number 1: Fear the Lord!

Additional Thoughts:

_____

_____

_____

_____

_____

_____

_____

_____

_____

APPLICATION:

Accentuate:

1. Planning. You are great here but plan to spend only the increase (interest) that you gain from your investments. Plan so that the principal remains. You are not spending the principal but you are only spending the interest.
2. Teach others to do what you have done. Help them learn how to make great financial decisions. Reach back.

Eliminate:

1. Comparisons! Don't compare yourself with someone else.
2. Judgment of others. Don't condemn assuming they should be in a better position. They may not have had the financial education you did; whether by the school of hard knocks or formal learning. So take the opportunity to inspire, encourage and not judge.
3. Don't throw your pearls before swine (Matthew 7:6). Don't spend time investing in opportunists to the detriment of yourself, your family or others. You want willing participants; invest where it's going to make the greatest impact and have the greatest influence.

Additional Thoughts:

_____
_____
_____
_____
_____
_____
_____
_____
_____

MINDSET:

Remain Kingdom minded! God knows everything we are going through. He is our provider. He is truly our source. Don't fall into the Fear Of Missing Out (FOMO). Don't fall into the You Only Live Once (YOLO) mentality. Don't fall into the desperate mindset or poverty, scarcity mindset as you get older. Just remember that God loves you and will look out for you 100%. Constantly renew your mind.

Boundaries need to be maintained. Large gifts especially to family and family members need to be carefully considered. You may need to set age limits on gifts to make sure it is adequately invested appropriately. For instance, when preparing a will with young children involved, you'll want to limit the amount of money and access to businesses until an age they can make rational decisions. You want to prepare them to make wise financial decisions; so they don't squander what you have worked so hard to gain. You should put boundaries in place stipulating age, educational or enterprise related only may be feasible.

Don't think that you know it all. Sometimes we think that we have arrived because we know more than someone else. Always remain humble and have a teachable spirit. There is always somebody who knows more. We are not Jacks of all trades or Jills either. We don't know everything and someone can always teach us something new so why not learn. To increase in knowledge, be a perpetual student.

Additional Thoughts:

_____

_____

_____

_____

_____

_____

_____

_____

GOAL SETTING:

1. Add those people whom you want to help. Pick a large number. In 2020, I wanted to reach 2020 individuals and influence them to have a better financial future; to change the economic footprint. Set a goal that is more of a reach than just increasing your own profit.
2. Plan to only spend your interest in retirement. Try to be ahead of the cost of living curve (aim for your percentage increases on investments to be greater than cost of living).
3. Determine your date to receive Social Security and distributions from your retirement accounts. RMD (Required Minimum Distribution) must start at the age of 70 ½. If you have enough to live on prior to then you can delay distributions until that date. Your goal should be to wait until as close to 70 ½ as possible.
4. Calculate how much money you will need or spend annually from your current age until 70 ½. This will help you set your goal.
5. Check for hidden fees in your portfolio. Managed mutual funds over time could cost you hundreds of thousands of dollars. www.personalcapital.com , www.personalfund.com/app/ www.portfoliocheckup.com are good places to start.

6. Consider index funds which are made up of a list of top stocks in that asset class. They offer "maximum diversification, minimal cost, and maximum tax efficiency, low turnover (trading), and low turnover cost, and no sales loads'" – '*Money: Master The Game*' by Tony Robbins.
7. Quarterly check your portfolio and rebalance, if necessary, twice a year.
8. Consider using a fiduciary. A registered investment advisor (RIA) will give unbiased advice and their fees could be tax deductible. The flat advice fee is conflict free. Be sure they are NOT affiliated with a broker (known as dual registration).
9. Have your estate plan evaluated. If you don't have one, get your affairs in order. Determine who will be the executor.
10. Document your digital assets and put them in a safe place. Make sure your executor has a copy or knows where to find them. Companies will not give out information for online accounts; it is important that they have your ID and password to access the account and make any changes.

Goals

- Financial Dreams
- Family Goals
- Future (Legacy) Goals

Goals (cont.)

Savings

Short Term

Debt Reduction

Long Term

Credit Score

Investing

Destined To Prosper

Additional Thoughts:

_____
_____
_____
_____
_____
_____

BUDGETING:

You have this area under control. You've been budgeting all along. Keep it up and keep evaluating. Look out for rising costs. The system is set to take as much of your money as possible. If you don't need the service or item any longer, cut it out. If costs keep rising, re-evaluate whether or not it is really something that you need.

Additional Thoughts:

_____
_____
_____
_____
_____
_____
_____

SAVING:

Evaluate your present savings and compare it to your investments for the future. Make sure you have enough for today and not just a whole lot for tomorrow. Continue to save so that you aren't dipping into what is earmarked for the future.

'Render unto Caesar the things which are Caesars' – Matthew 22:21

Withholdings	Actual	Budgeted	Notes:
Federal Income Tax			
State Income Tax			
City Income Tax			
FICA			
Medical Insurance			
Dental Insurance			
Vision Insurance			
Health Savings Account (FSA/HSA)			
401(k)			
Total Withholdings			

'Rich rule over the poor and the borrower is slave to the lender' Proverbs 22:7

Finance Payments	Actual	Budgeted
Credit Card 1		
Credit Card 2		
Credit Card 3		
Credit Card 4		
Student loan		
Auto Loan/ Car Payment		
Home Mortgage		
Personal loan		
Total Finance Payments		

Constantly look for opportunities to save more or to have a higher interest rate. Consider online accounts that pay more interest than the local bank or a money market account. I'm sure you are not paying a monthly maintenance fee for having an account. If you are, eliminate it. Constantly look for opportunities where you can have a higher increase, sometimes banks create special accounts requiring you to transfer a certain dollar amount for a specified time. The promise may be to give you a cash reward, usually a lot more interest than you would have gained. Be on the look out for those opportunities.

Additional Thoughts:

_____

_____

_____

_____

_____

_____

_____

_____

DEBT REDUCTION:

If you do still have debt, you want to pay it off as quickly as possible. Be strategic. As an example: relating to mortgages; instead of paying monthly pay bi-weekly. Split the payment in half and pay every two weeks. You end up saving on interest and paying off your mortgage a lot sooner. Systematically look at what you are spending and where you have debt, so that you can reduce it and truly be financially free.

Additional Thoughts:

_____
_____
_____
_____
_____
_____
_____
_____
_____

CONTEMPLATION:

Here are some questions to consider:

1. What are some of the miraculous blessings God has done for you?

   _____
   _____
   _____
   _____
   _____

2. How can you bless others in the same way?

   _____
   _____
   _____
   _____
   _____

3. Who mentored you along your path to financial prosperity?

   _____
   _____
   _____
   _____
   _____

4. Who can you mentor? How can you pay it forward?

   _____
   _____
   _____
   _____
   _____

5. What is your next goal?

   _____
   _____
   _____
   _____
   _____

6. How can you continue to be a conduit for God?

   _____
   _____
   _____
   _____
   _____

7. What limits do you have on God's plans for you?

_____
_____
_____
_____
_____

Additional Thoughts:

_____
_____
_____
_____
_____
_____
_____
_____
_____
_____

LIFE LESSONS:

When you are Financially Free and Retiring Early (FIRE) everybody want to seek you out. They come out of the woodwork so that they can ask to borrow from you.

A friend and I recognized many were coming to us asking for assistance. We prepared for the future but were cognizant that current resources can be squandered by being so merciful and kind hearted. My friend purchased several copies of my book "Financial Wisdom For Financial Freedom", a do it yourself book that takes you through budgeting, saving, debt reduction, credit, etc. When others asked to borrow money, she loaned it to them but also gave them a book. She was willing to teach them to put their finances in order. Most of the requestors never came back to her again. She did allow the word of God, which is steeped in the book, as well as the instructions and applications to assist them in what can sometimes be the slow process of growth.

Additionally, I've had the opportunity to not only write "Financial Wisdom For Financial Freedom" but also "Not Just Paper", which gives the theology and theory side. I've had the privilege to teach Biblical Finance for over 15 years assisting students in renewing their mind in relationship with money. It is a culmination of the years of teaching, and is used in many Christian colleges and universities. Home schoolers and Christian high schools use it to ensure that the youth understand what the word of God says as it relates to finances. A devotional planner, "Divinely Connected: Steps to Fearless Financial Freedom" is also available to aid in taking small systematic steps toward financial peace. There are many options so don't keep the information to yourself but be willing to share and use it to propel others.

A client was forced to retire early. Though she had been saving for a long time she was forced to re-evaluate her investments. She needed to identify her current financial state in relation to her needs. Retiring in your 50's isn't normal when we are programmed to wait until our 60's. She was concerned that Social Security wouldn't be available until she was 62 at the earliest. She had no designated beneficiaries. In talking with her, we devised a plan based on her needs. Taking her current age to the age of 62, we calculated how much money she was spending annually and multiplied by the years until 62 (if you have a monthly amount then multiply it by twelve first to get the annual). She discovered she was only two years short of what she would need in liquid cash.

We then evaluated how much she would be getting monthly in Social Security, to determine if it was going to be sufficient to live on until her 70's. Though she hadn't worked the 35 years (she had 31) that Social Security uses to calculate distribution amounts, she made significantly enough to warrant a large enough distribution. She determined that if she could work for 4 additional years then she would maximize her Social Security distribution. However, her distribution with 31 years was more than sufficient; she really didn't have to work. She only needed to fill that gap of 2 years prior to receiving any distribution. She had options: she could be a contract employee; invest or start a business; or she could maximize the interest she gained on her cash liquid accounts to make up the difference. She had everything she needed for retirement, she just needed to fill that two year gap. She is financially independent retiring early (FIRE). She is also financially free by using wisdom, and helping others. She's not just giving them a fish sandwich but she's teaching them how to fish. She has it all together, burning bright and helping others start their fire. **IGNITE THE FIRE.**

Additional Thoughts:

_____
_____
_____
_____
_____
_____
_____
_____
_____

CHRISTIAN ENTREPRENEURS:

As business owners, God has a great plan for you! You are running it for the Kingdom impact. First let's commit all of our ways unto the Lord so that our business and our plans will be established and they will succeed (Proverbs 16:3)

As we relate your financial personality to your business, here's my admonition:

> Get your personal finances in order. It can't be assumed that as a Christian entrepreneur you have your personal finances together. 99% of the time they are not in order and it shows up in our business.

Suggestions that will move the needle and skyrocket your business; your personality might be holding you back.

STEAM: (Spend Thinking Emotionally About Memories)

This is the person that is always giving. You may be doing the same thing in your business. Look at your bottom line; you're likely to find that you are not making as much profit as you should. Why? Many fall into the same category, we love what we do and we want to help God's people. We want to show up as light in a dark world. Often we are giving away our services for free. We are treating it more like a hobby and not like a business.

Tips:
1. Get an assistant; virtual or a physical person in your office. Identify them to handle the financial end of transactions. Why? Because you would give it away for free. They will make sure you have income.
2. Select a point person that will collect the funds for the service or product that you sell. Allow them to take your payment before services are rendered.
3. Check your website. It is important and imperative at the start of a business that you talk to your customers and walk them through the selection process of your offerings. You want them to come to know, like and trust you. Typically, what we show on our business page (or website) is a free consultation. Shorten it especially after you have been established. Why? Because you are giving away your hourly rate for free. Many people are looking out for themselves. They take up your time to sell their wares to you and because you have a heart to give, often you buy. You have taken away your opportunity to increase your revenue.

Get an assistant, put them in charge of receiving the money. Make sure that they capture it before you start giving services. Also, look at your website and reduce your availability. Yes, community service and giving are good but make sure to identify that ahead of time. Put profits first. Paid work comes before housework and free work.

Additional Thoughts:

_____

_____

_____

_____

_____

_____

_____

WATER: (Why Attend To Every Report)

This is the person who doesn't want to pay attention to the details and the number crunching. Business is a numbers game and you need to know your numbers. Positioning and pricing products appropriately leads to profits and succeeding. Barely making ends meet is not what God desires. Don't give it all away.

Suggestions:

1. Get an accountant. Find a book keeper, who can track weekly income and expenses. Once set, you will need to maintain the process. Set quarterly or monthly meetings to stay on top of all your finances and make adjustments as necessary.

2. Look at your profit margin. Do you have profit built into your pricing for your products. If not, make the correction to adequately reflect your value. You need income. Once corrected you'll start seeing the increases and the profits rise. You really are worth it.

Income and profit allow you to impact the Kingdom. Money is simply a tool to use in this world. Shine so that you can influence, impact and invest in the right places.

Additional Thoughts:

_____
_____
_____
_____
_____
_____
_____
_____
_____

ICE: (I Can't Entertain)

This personality is on the saving side of the equation. Budgets are in order; finances are set but appreciation and celebration are lacking. As a Christian business owner, you may be missing opportunities in employee and customer relations.

Suggestion:

Survey your employees. Consider the other side. Acknowledge the value they bring to the business and how you can appreciate them. Appreciate those that are working for you as well as those that you have the opportunity to work with. Gift employees and customers to show appreciation. If profit is low a small token or a card will suffice. A raise, a gift, product or service that you normally would charge for could be an excellent gift. Give something of value that melts your ICE personality. It also allows them to warm up to you. They will appreciate you later.

Additional Thoughts:

_____
_____
_____
_____
_____
_____
_____

FIRE: (Financially Independent Retiring Early)

The difference between ICE and FIRE is that the FIRE personality is already appreciating their customers and employees consistently. These are the bosses that are walking not only in integrity but also in love. They are giving an honest days work for an honest days pay. They are also appreciating those that are working hard. They are enthusiastic positive motivators that move mountains. They are leaders.

Suggestions:
1. Balance. Make sure you are investing in the employees. Put balance in place; you have it in your life also have it in your business. Make sure you're appreciating and investing in them.
2. Sign up for a 401K or investment instrument where employees can make contributions. Maybe you are at a point where you can invest a portion. You may be able to match up to a certain percentage. Begin offering a health care plan. You are investing in your employees and they will do a better job.
3. Consider investing in their financial education to improve their money management skills and quit complaining about wages. They would recognize the blessing of income and make better financial decisions. They will be content.

It has been my privilege to work with many entrepreneurs in many types of businesses. Group coaching for entrepreneurs is ideal because pivoting your business may be required depending on the climate. This mastermind atmosphere allows like-minded individuals to assist with valuable expertise. This wisdom reduces the time it takes for a business to recover. Others can offer an outside eye to give great tips for improvement.

The financial personality you have is important, review them and utilize the tools as it relates to business.

Additional Thoughts:

_____

_____

_____

_____

_____

_____

_____

_____

_____

COUPLES:

As we come together to be one, the financial area poses a great concern. Statistics show that in the top three reasons for divorce, money issues are always present. Aside from premarital counseling, couples counseling/coaching on this topic can bridge the gap in thinking. Understanding your personality and that of your spouse allows for creating a workable relationship.

2 STEAM

Two spenders. Caution on all cylinders. Both want to give but wisdom must be used as well as the word 'NO'.

1. Select the person to handle the bills
2. Create a balanced budget jointly so each person understands the financial situation.
3. Set up automatic deductions for the bills, from the joint account.
4. Consider having separate spending accounts. This would be their ability to bless others. Each person will access and be responsible for maintaining his or her account.

Additional Thoughts:

_____
_____
_____
_____
_____
_____
_____
_____

2 WATER

Two avoiders. Someone has to step up and take charge of this ship. Necessities must come before adventure.

1. Select the person to handle the bills or decide to alternate monthly or quarterly.
2. Determine the method for budgeting (spreadsheet or envelope)
3. Create a balanced budget. Journal to ensure accuracy.
4. Embrace the adventurous and fun loving side and celebrate that within the boundary.

Additional Thoughts:

_____
_____
_____
_____
_____
_____
_____
_____
_____

2 ICE

Two savers mean you are on track for the future.

1. Review your budget and add some fun.
2. Hold each other accountable to identify fun items each week. Set a dollar amount if you like but plan your fun.

Additional Thoughts:

_____
_____
_____
_____
_____
_____
_____
_____

2 FIRE

Two security driven bosses. You are a power couple and rocking your financial future.

Invest in each other. Focus on your partner and suggest investment opportunities (education, business, etc.)

Additional Thoughts:

_____
_____
_____
_____
_____
_____
_____
_____
_____

STEAM & WATER

Combinations are to be celebrated. Move past frustration and highlight the good qualities.

1. Have the STEAM in charge of the bill paying.
2. Ask the WATER to set the limits for giving.
3. Encourage the STEAM to do something for themselves.
4. Balance the budget with WATER present and paying attention.

Additional Thoughts:

_____
_____
_____
_____
_____
_____
_____
_____
_____

STEAM & ICE

The best of both worlds in balance.

1. Have ICE create the budget and track spending.
2. Give STEAM an allowance for gift giving.
3. Separate accounts for fun or future but the bill account is off limits.

Additional Thoughts:

_____
_____
_____
_____
_____
_____
_____
_____
_____
_____

STEAM & FIRE

Same as STEAM & ICE

WATER & ICE

The clash of the goals but accentuate the giftings.

1. Have ICE create the budget with input from WATER
2. Have ICE teach WATER about money management and show the decision making process.
3. Allow WATER to suggest the fun activities and allot for it in the budget.
4. WATER is responsible to get ICE to play.

Additional Thoughts:

_____
_____
_____
_____
_____
_____
_____
_____

WATER & FIRE

Same as WATER & ICE

ICE & FIRE

From better to best and moving toward excellent. You are really on the same page. Risk temperament may vary in investing.

1. Collaborate on the budget.
2. Have FIRE explain the long-term goals and focus. Identify all securities and investments. Teach ICE your planning model.
3. Invest in each other and force the fun.

Collaboration is key. For ICE and FIRE accentuate and celebrate the future focus and attention to detail. For STEAM and WATER accentuate and celebrate the giving and enjoyment in life.

Additional Thoughts:

_____

_____

_____

_____

_____

_____

_____

_____

_____

_____

Financial Assessment:

- ☐ Written Financial Goal – Y/N
- ☐ Written Family Goal – Y/N
- ☐ Balanced Budget – Y/N
- ☐ Cash $ _____
- ☐ Emergency Fund $ _____
- ☐ Savings $ _____
- ☐ Debt $ _____
- ☐ Credit Score _____
- ☐ Investments $ _____
- ☐ Net Worth $ _____

TO DO:

_____
_____
_____
_____
_____
_____

APPENDIX:

Additional Scriptures for Meditation:

John 10:10

Proverbs 13:22

Deuteronomy 24:10-17

Proverbs 11:15

Proverbs 17:18

Proverbs 22:26

Proverbs 6:1-5

Psalm 37:21

Leviticus 19:23

Exodus 22:14

Deuteronomy 15:6

Deuteronomy 28:12

Proverbs 22:7

Romans 13:8

Proverbs 13:11

Genesis 12:2

Goals (cont.)

Savings _____

_____

_____

_____

_____

Short Term

Debt Reduction

_____

_____

_____

_____

_____

Long Term

Credit Score

_____

_____

_____

_____

Investing _____

_____

_____

_____

_____

Income:	Actual	Budgeted	Notes:
Salary 1			
Salary 2			
Investment			
Stocks and Bonds			
Alimony			
Child Support			
Other			
Total Income			

'Render unto Caesar the things which are Caesars' – Matthew 22:21

Withholdings	Actual	Budgeted	Notes:
Federal Income Tax			
State Income Tax			
City Income Tax			
FICA			
Medical Insurance			
Dental Insurance			
Vision Insurance			
Health Savings Account (FSA/HSA)			
401(k)			
Total Withholdings			

'Rich rule over the poor and the borrower is slave to the lender' Proverbs 22:7

Finance Payments	Actual	Budgeted	
Credit Card 1			
Credit Card 2			
Credit Card 3			
Credit Card 4			
Student loan			
Auto Loan/ Car Payment			
Home Mortgage			
Personal loan			
Total Finance Payments			

Credit Score Highlight &Goals

- Payment History: # of late payments _____
- Amount owed: _____
  (this is your total debt)
- % Utilization: _____
  (Amount owed/Total limit x 100%)
- Length of credit history: _____
  (how long you have had credit)
- Derogatory marks: _____
  Date to remove: _____

- Current Score _____

	Goal
	0
	$0
	0%
	The longer the better
	0
	700+

52 Week Money Challenge

Week	Deposit Amount	Account Balance	Week	Deposit Amount	Account Balance
1	1.00	$1.00	27	27.00	$378.00
2	2.00	$3.00	28	28.00	$406.00
3	3.00	$6.00	29	29.00	$435.00
4	4.00	$10.00	30	30.00	$465.00
5	5.00	$15.00	31	31.00	$496.00
6	6.00	$21.00	32	32.00	$528.00
7	7.00	$28.00	33	33.00	$561.00
8	8.00	$36.00	34	34.00	$595.00
9	9.00	$45.00	35	35.00	$630.00
10	10.00	$55.00	36	36.00	$666.00
11	11.00	$66.00	37	37.00	$703.00
12	12.00	$78.00	38	38.00	$741.00
13	13.00	$91.00	39	39.00	$780.00
14	14.00	$105.00	40	40.00	$820.00
15	15.00	$120.00	41	41.00	$861.00
16	16.00	$136.00	42	42.00	$903.00
17	17.00	$153.00	43	43.00	$946.00
18	18.00	$171.00	44	44.00	$990.00
19	19.00	$190.00	45	45.00	$1,035.00
20	20.00	$210.00	46	46.00	$1,081.00
21	21.00	$231.00	47	47.00	$1,128.00
22	22.00	$253.00	48	48.00	$1,176.00
23	23.00	$276.00	49	49.00	$1,225.00
24	24.00	$300.00	50	50.00	$1,275.00
25	25.00	$325.00	51	51.00	$1,326.00
26	26.00	$351.00	52	52.00	$1,378.00

FREE	29	32	16	4	24	18	8	31
9	43	5	23	38	7	1	41	3
42	15	27	52	47	49	28	22	34
25	37	19	46	FREE	45	26	19	29
11	13	35	50	48	51	14	44	2
33	39	21	39	17	12	36	6	40

Though you can follow the 52 week savings table each week for the year, I suggest you use it like bingo and put in the maximum you have that week. The Bingo table is shown above. For instance, though it may be the 1st week of the year but you received an unexpected gift of $50 then put in the $50 and mark that week as complete. If you have enough to cover more than one of the weeks at the higher level, then do so. This means with interest you can save more. This also allows you to work backwards and when the end of the year comes you won't feel strapped about saving $52 that week, instead you will only need $1. The options are many: start at $1 and each week save the designated amount; begin at the end of the chart and work backwards; or use the chart like bingo and deposit the maximum you have available.

Debt Snowball   The wicked borrow and do not repay – Psalm 37:21

Company	Debt owed	Interest Rate	Term of Loan	Minimum Payment	Amount Paying
1.					
2.					
3.					
4.					
5.					

Links to accelerate your financial freedom:

Missing money: www.usa.gov and www.missingmoney.com

Unclaimed property: www.unclaimed.org

Unclaimed assets: www.fiscal.treasury.gov

Check your investment performance: www.moneychimp.com/features/portfolio_performance_calculator.htm

www.moneychimp.com/calculator (for other financial calculators)

Check for hidden mutual fund fees: www.personalcapital.com

www.portfoliocheckup.com

www.personalfund.com/app

Online Course:

Financialopoly: Financial Wisdom For Financial Freedom: https://bit.ly/H2Hfincourse

Looking for your next step to gain total financial success? https://bit.ly/H2Hstrategy

Also available:

Family Worship:
Reaching All Who Attend   ISBN 9781436370158

Financial Wisdom For Financial Freedom
                             ISBN 9780999173305
                             ISBN 9780999173312

Not Just Paper   ISBN 9780999173329
                            ISBN 9780999173336

Divinely Connected: Steps to Fearless Financial Freedom
                            ISBN 9780999173343
                            ISBN 9780999173350

Divinely Connected: Sister 2 Sister
                            ISBN 9780999173381
                            ISBN 9781736395905

Divinely Connected: Praying Through Life's Struggles
                            ISBN 9780999173398
                            ISBN 9781736395912

DIVINELY CONNECTED SERIES

Heart 2 Heart Truth Ministries H2HTruth.org

DR. CHONTA T. A. HAYNES

Devotional Planners to keep you connected. Reflection and introspection lead to revelation and acceleration.

PICK UP OR DOWNLOAD YOUR COPY TODAY!

Https://bit.ly/H2Hdevo

Taking you on a journey to transform your finances

PICK UP OR DOWNLOAD YOUR COPY TODAY!

Https://bit.ly/H2Hbundle

Courses designed to guide you to the next level at your pace and when you are ready.

REGISTER TODAY!

Https://bit.ly/H2Hcourses

ABOUT THE AUTHOR

Dr. Chonta Haynes has an exciting, inviting, encouraging, fire cracker personality in Biblical teaching. Uncompromising when it comes to the word of God, she is passionate to help believers live an abundant life by putting feet to their faith. She pours her heart into God's word seeking treasures to share with others. Dr. Haynes is a compassionate relationship builder and communicator skilled in meeting spiritual needs through education, coaching and motivation. She believes true learning and transformation is not head to head but heart to heart.

Her experiences include Academic Operations Officer, Theology and Christian Education professor, youth coordinator, lead Chaplain as well as author of *"Family Worship: Reaching All Who Attend"*, *"Financial Wisdom For Financial Freedom"*, *"Not Just Paper"*, and *"Divinely Connected: Steps to Fearless Financial Freedom"*. She holds a Bachelor's degree in Electrical Engineering from Georgia Institute of Technology and a Master's degree in the same subject from the University of Miami (FL). She has a Bachelor of Arts, Master of Arts and Ph. D in Theology from Life Christian University and a Christian Counseling degree from Grace & Truth Christian University.

Your Biblical money management expert and Amazon bestselling author, she remains a perpetual student in order to bring a fresh word.

www.H2HTruth.org

Podcast – heart2hearttruth

www.linkedin.com/in/chonta-haynes
www.instagram.com/ctahaynes
www.pinterest.com/chontah/messages
www.facebook.com/chonta.haynes
www.facebook.com/h2htruth
www.twitter.com/chonta_haynes

Heart 2 Heart Truth Foundation 501 (c) 3

God has provided opportunities to meet the needs of others and bring the Gospel in a practical way. Dr. Haynes' books have been distributed through the library system, churches and Christian colleges to serve the larger population.

Prayers: Take the challenge of 7 days asking God for divine intervention.

Sign up at https://bit.ly/H2Hprayer

Scan for specials, events and extras

www.ingramcontent.com/pod-product-compliance
Lightning Source LLC
Chambersburg PA
CBHW070550010526
44118CB00012B/1283